S.S. EAGLE

The Secret Mission
1944-45

S.S. EAGLE

The Secret Mission 1944-45

Harold Squires

Jesperson Press Limited
1992

Jesperson Press Limited
39 James Lane
St. John's, NF, Canada
A1E 3H3

Design, Printing and Binding: Jesperson Press Limited
Cover Design: Jesperson Press Limited

The publisher acknowledges a financial contribution from the *Cultural Affairs Division* of the *Department of Culture, Recreation and Youth* of the Government of Newfoundland and Labrador which has helped make this publication possible.

Appreciation is also expressed to the *Canada Council* for its assistance in publishing this work.

Canadian Cataloguing in Publication Data

Squires, Harold, 1923-

SS Eagle
ISBN 0-921692-37-4

I. Title.

PS8587.Q57S73 1992 C813'.54 C92-098701-X
PR9199.3S68S73 1992

The publisher is grateful to the Provincial Archives for providing some of the photographs and maps used.

This book is dedicated to the captain and crew of that gallant old ship, the S.S. Eagle *who sailed her to the Antarctic and back to her home port, St. John's, Newfoundland, 1944-45.*

Foreword

Radio Officer Harold Squires has delegated the honour to me of explaining in ordinary terms the importance of accurate timekeeping on board a ship.

On joining the *Eagle* Hal Squires was asked by Captain Robert Sheppard to arrange some means of passing radio time signals from the wireless room, aft on the deck, to the chart room (the skipper's bedroom), down below amidships. To accomplish this, Hal rigged a bell with a pushbutton but was so impressed with Sheppard's attention to timekeeping arrangements that some brief explanation of its necessity was in order. The *Eagle* had been employed in the Newfoundland seal fishery where such niceties as a time signal bell and a chart room were considered unnecessary.

For the benefit of non-seafaring readers, accurate time-keeping is not essential to determining latitude. Early ocean navigators knew that the Pole Star appeared to be stationary in the heavens. As one proceeds northward the Pole Star rises higher. As one goes southward the star appears lower in the sky until at the equator it is on the horizon. The angle of elevation of the Pole Star above the horizon corresponds to the ship's latitude. Similarly, with the sun, latitude can be obtained by observing the highest altitude the sun reaches at noon and reference to elementary tables giving the sun's angular distance north or south of the equator. For centuries navigators determined latitude without reference to clocks.

Not so with longitude. Accurate time is necessary to calculate longitude from observations. Longitude was determined by keeping account of the estimated distance a ship covered east or west from the known longitude of the ship's departure point. The longitude assumed after weeks of sailing could be in error by hundreds of miles. Mariners and indeed nations were well aware of the problem of "finding the longitude". Spain and Holland offered prizes for a solution. The problem hinged on accurate timekeeping, and existing clocks did not have the required accuracy. Clockmakers and scientists such as Sir Isaac Newton declared the task to be impossible.

In the early 1700s the British Parliament created a Board of Longitude. This body offered a prize of £10,000 for a method of determining longitude within 60 miles after a voyage of six weeks out of sight of land. The award was to be increased to £15,000 if correct to within 40 miles and to £20,000 if within 30 miles of the true longitude.

A craftsman named John Harrison worked some 30 years completing four successive timekeepers. The number four watch easily passed the sea trial on a voyage to Jamaica. However, the Board of Longitude, instead of paying Harrison the top award started a long argument with Harrison, demanding a scientific explanation as to why the watch was so accurate. When Harrison was eighty years old, with active help from King George III, he was finally paid the top award with some deductions.

The importance of dependable and accurate chronometers probably reached its zenith during the era of Captain Cook's voyages of exploration and his charting of the unknown parts of the seas. After Harrison, clockmakers constructed superb timekeepers with a constant rate of error one second a day for months. With no means of checking it after departure, it was considered the most precious item on the ship, guarded and cared for accordingly. With the advent of wireless and the broadcasting of time signals the navigator became much more confident because he could check his clock daily. Today the error in advanced quartz clocks for navigation is virtually nil but the need for such clocks has almost disappeared. Conventional navigation is being rapidly replaced by electronic systems which display the ship's position.

Hal and I sailed on the *Eagle* on a sealing voyage in 1948. One of my most vivid memories is of standing a safe distance outside the wireless shack watching Hal and his colleague operator, Rod Roberts, operating the spark transmitter with the frightful cracks of the spark gap. The door of the shack was always open, no doubt to let the ozone escape — possibly also, to let the operators escape if necessary.

— *Captain William Hancock*

ACKNOWLEDGEMENTS

I would like to acknowledge and give thanks to Mr. Mike McCarthy who helped me with my manuscript.

Also, I would like to express my deepest gratitude to Mr. Wilson Lewis, recently deceased, whose persistent persuasion prompted me to write this true story.

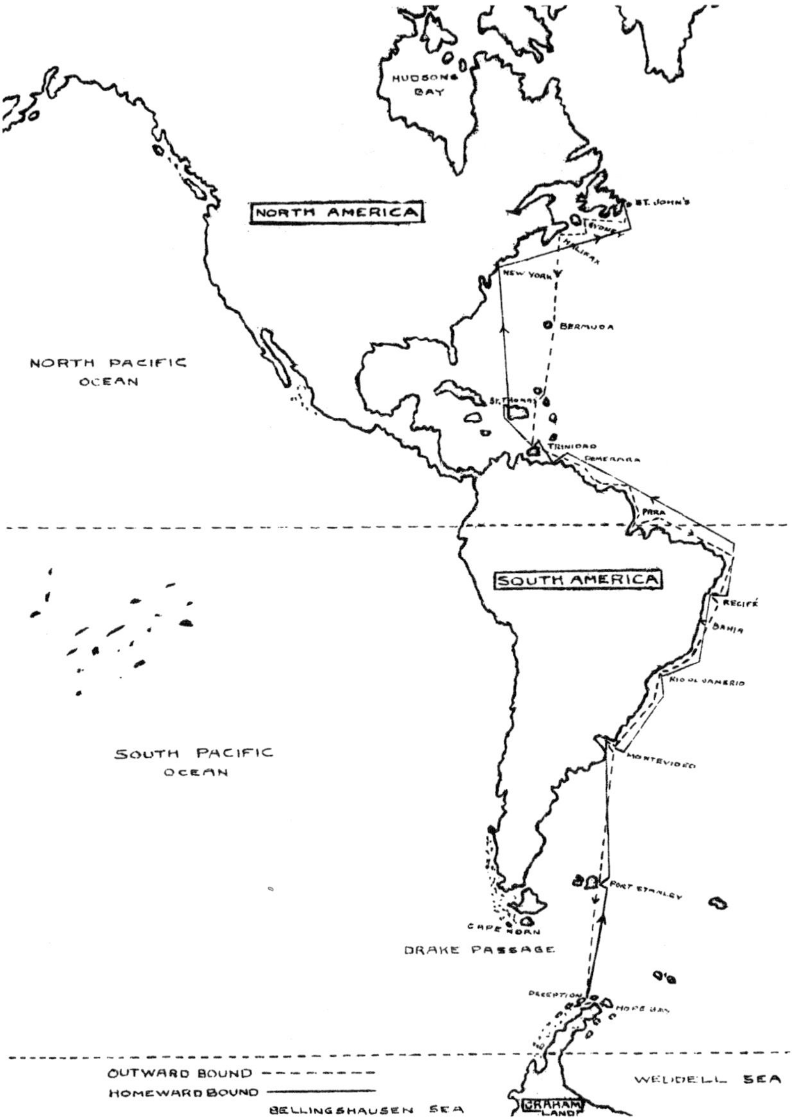

This map was taken from the official photographic record of the voyage.

PREFACE

Newfoundlanders, at least most of them, are unaware that their province has contributed to the history of the Falklands in Britain's battle with Argentina for sovereignty over regions in the southern hemisphere.

In 1943, while the outcome of World War II was still undecided, Great Britain resumed pre-war research and development in the Falkland Islands Dependencies. The main objectives of the Falkland Islands Dependencies Survey was to complete the mapping of Graham Land started by J.R. Rymill's British Graham Land Expedition in 1935 and 1936, to set up wireless weather stations and to carry out a detailed economic survey of the area.

The real purpose went well beyond the stated objectives. The Falkland Islands Dependencies, which consisted of islands off the northern tip of Graham Land and parts of Antarctica itself, had been brought under British control in 1908 and 1917. But to secure British sovereignty, colonization was deemed necessary. The voyages, beginning in 1943, were designed to serve this function. You may well wonder why Great Britain, with a global war on its hands, would select this time to inhabit the cold, desolate Antarctic wastelands. It was probably because the Antarctic Peninsula had a geological make-up favourable for great deposits of copper, lead, zinc, gold, silver and other minerals useful in war-time.

The main purpose of the first voyage, to establish bases in the South Shetlands and on the Trinity Peninsula, was not achieved because the vessels, the S.S. *Fitzroy* and H.M.S. *William Scoresby*, chartered by the British Admiralty were unsuitable and could not get through the pack-ice in the Antarctic Sound. In January 1944, the vessels sailed from Port Stanley and shortly thereafter established a base at Deception Island. They then set sail for Hope Bay planning to establish a second base, however a belt of pack-ice blocked the entrance to the bay. The *William Scoresby* did succeed in landing a party, but the *Fitzroy* which carried the hut and supplies for the base could not penetrate the ice. It was then decided that Port Lockroy should become the temporary base.

Frustrated and disappointed in their attempt to establish a permanent main base in Hope Bay, the British Admiralty decided to try again the next season. It was in Newfoundland that the British found the one remaining ship which could do the job, the S.S. *Eagle*, the last of Newfoundland's wooden sealing steamers.

The *Eagle* was chartered by the British Admiralty from Bowring's in St. John's, and Captain Robert C. Sheppard was chosen to take command. He commissioned the *Eagle* in only two weeks, giving up his job as Harbour Master to do so. He was confident that he and his hand-picked crew of twenty-eight Newfoundlanders could take the *Eagle* to Hope Bay on its secret mission, known as Operation "Tabarin". The objectives of the survey were to relieve the party at Deception Island, where the meteorological station was to be continued, to construct shelter on Coronation Island for the next year and to transfer men from Port Lockroy to Hope Bay on the north-eastern tip of Graham Land. It was hoped that Hope Bay would become the main base for mapping the east coast of Graham Land. Most of the west coast had been mapped in earlier years by Rymill's expedition.

On October 24, 1944, the *Eagle* set sail for the Falklands. Three months and 8,000 miles later, she arrived in Port Stanley, the capital of the Falklands.

Truly an epic story of a wooden ship and iron men.

Chapter 1

I first went to sea as a boy of seventeen in 1940. It was an exciting time to serve in the Merchant Marine, for German submarines haunted the North Atlantic sea lanes, and every voyage was fraught with danger. This was especially true of the slow, old cargo ships I served on. Their inability to maintain speed in heavy weather made it difficult to stay in convoy under the protection of escorting naval vessels. Alone, with no naval or air protection they soon became sitting ducks for the enemy submarines. However, on at least one occasion, the slow speed of the ship I was serving on saved us from a deadly encounter with the enemy.

It was the fall of 1944, and I was serving as Wireless Officer on the S.S. *Moyra,* an old cargo vessel chartered by the Newfoundland Railway. We were outward bound on a voyage from New York to Halifax, when a brisk, northerly wind caused us to lag behind our convoy. Seeing that he could not maintain enough speed to keep in convoy, our captain decided to chart a different course to Halifax than that taken by the convoy. We arrived safely in port, but soon learned that on the night that we had dropped behind, the convoy had been badly mauled by enemy submarines with a great loss of lives and ships.

It was on this voyage from New York to Halifax that I made up my mind to seek a berth as Wireless Officer on a larger, faster ship. So, when we later arrived in St. John's, Newfoundland, I left the *Moyra*. With no suitable berth available in St. John's, I returned to Halifax, found lodgings at the Merchant Navy Officers' Hostel, and registered with the British Manning Pool.

Two days later I was called to the British Manning Pool and asked to serve on a top secret mission. I agreed, and was immediately issued a first-class ticket, and told to travel back to St. John's and report to Captain James C. Grieve of the Ministry of Transport for further orders.

When I boarded the train in Halifax I was unaware that I was embarking on the first step of what was to be the most exciting and memorable voyage of my life on one of the last truly great ships of the old Newfoundland sealing fleet.

Now, as the last surviving member of the officers and crew who sailed on that top secret assignment, I would like to pass on the story of that great voyage when the S.S. *Eagle* went south.

CHAPTER 2

I was very curious about the secret mission I was to serve on, but Captain Grieve said very little about it. My orders were to report to Captain Robert G. Sheppard of the S.S. *Eagle*, then docked at Bowring's wharf on the Southside of St. John's. I made my way to the Southside and found the S.S. *Eagle*. My first impression of the sealing ship was of an old, dirty, black-wooden steamer, with a clipper bow and a cargo barrel in her foretop. I went on board and asked to see Captain Sheppard.

Captain Sheppard told me he was happy to have me as a member of his crew, and then quickly briefed me on the voyage we were to make on the S.S. *Eagle*. He had been selected just two weeks earlier by the British Admiralty to take the old sealing ship on a voyage to Antarctica on behalf of the British Government.

Having revealed where the voyage of the S.S. *Eagle* was to take us, and why, Captain Sheppard turned me over to Mr. Tom Carroll, the Third Officer of the ship, to show me to the wireless room. Skipper Tom, as he was called because of his age and experience, was a grand old man of eighty-one years who had sailed with Captain Bob Bartlett on the Perry expedition of 1908-09.

Captain Robert G. Sheppard, M.B.E.

Skipper Tom had a great deal of natural dignity and spoke with the soft accent of his Irish ancestors. "So you're our new Marconi man," he said when Captain Sheppard introduced us. "All right Markie follow me," and he led the way out of the captain's cabin.

"Markie?" I wondered why he didn't call me Sparks or Sparkie, the usual nicknames for a wireless operator, and asked him the reason for the strange name.

"I always call the wireless man, Markie," he said, "it's short for Marconi Man." So, Markie I remained until the end of our great adventure.

Skipper Tom led me up a small companion-way which took us to an elevated hutch abaft the funnel.

"I don't think you're going to like what you'll see, Markie," he said, as he searched in his pocket for the key to the wireless room. "I got an idea it's not quite what you've been used to, this door has been closed for quite a while."

I knew what he meant. The last voyage of the S.S.*Eagle* had been to the seal-hunt in April 1944 and it was now October of the same year. He finally found the key and I braced myself for the inevitable as the door swung open.

We stepped inside, and were greeted by the cold, musty, damp smell of a room that had not been aired for a long time. I immediately saw that the storage batteries were in need of immediate recharging and there was also the need for a proper ventilating system. It was quite clear that I had my work cut out to get things back in working order.

Skipper Tom then showed me my sleeping quarters in an adjoining cubby-hole. "Not much at the moment, is it Markie? But never mind, it'll look different after a fresh coat of paint, and the Captain has ordered new mattresses and pillows for all hands." With these reassuring words he left me to contemplate my new domain.

After Skipper Tom's departure I took a careful look at my sleeping quarters. There was a good ship's bunk on the forward wall with several drawers under it for storing personal belongings. The bunk was different from those of most ship bunks in that it headed port to starboard, instead of fore and aft. Later I found out that my bunk was the only one on the ship that didn't go fore and aft. In good nautical terms, it was "thwart ship".

The next thing that caught my eye was a small wooden box built into the deck. When I opened it I saw that the ship's steering chains passed under the floor of my cabin. Later I learned that the box was there so that the steering chain could be oiled easily. At first the noise of the steering chain disturbed me, but that soon passed, and after a few days at sea I didn't even hear it anymore.

The next thing I did was to carefully examine the wireless set. My heart sank when I saw the obsolete equipment I would have to work with. The old one hundred watts Sparks transmitter, with a maximum signal range of about two hundred miles under ideal weather conditions, was about the oldest wireless gear still in use on ships. Its signal tone was M.C.W. which was very low and usually around static level. The Captain would have to be told of the sad condition of the wireless room.

A check on the sanitary arrangements showed them to be very primitive. The S.S. *Eagle* was not fitted with plumbing. My bathroom facilities were a white enamel pan sunk in the counter shelf of the battery storage room, together with a soap dish and a small mirror. It was the same arrangement for all the officers and men. After having made a full survey of the wireless room and my sleeping quarters, I decided to explore the rest of the ship.

Chapter 3

I found my way to the saloon, and as it was empty I had a chance to look over the area. A long table ran the length of the room, which was heated by a large, upright hall stove, bolted to the deck with long rods. The stove was lit, and with the amount of heat it was throwing off I felt we didn't need to worry about low temperatures in Antarctica.

Next, I had a look at the captain's cabin. The cabin was small, and a new chart table being built by the carpenters took up a good deal of its space. It would be in this room that Captain Sheppard would do most of his chart work during our long voyage down the coast of South America to the South Pole.

Across from the captain's cabin was another small cabin with two bunks. I later learned that they were for the second officer and chief steward. A steward's pantry was next to this cabin.

Just aft of the captain's cabin, and not too far from the stove, I found the only flush toilet on the ship. It flushed by means of an overhead tank that was filled with a hand pump, and was strictly for ship's officers only. The crew had their own rather rough facilities on either side of the forecastle entrance—one for the deckhands, and one for the oilers and firemen.

Having looked things over I came back to the saloon. I sat down at the long table and ran over in my mind what I knew about the history of the S.S. *Eagle*. She was the second Newfoundland sealing ship to bear the name *Eagle* and measured one hundred seventy-six feet from stem to stern, had a net tonnage of four hundred and eighteen tons, and was powered by an 82 N.H.P. horsepower steam engine. Built in Norway in 1902, she was originally launched as the S.S. *Sophie*. A year later, in 1903, the ship was purchased by Bowring Brothers of St. John's to prosecute the annual Newfoundland seal-hunt. On arrival in St. John's she was renamed the S.S. *Eagle*. Now forty-two years old, and the veteran of as many trips to the ice, the S.S. *Eagle* was the last of the great, old, wooden-walled sealing steamers that still went to the ice.

I remembered as a small boy first hearing the name of the S.S. *Eagle* on the "Doyle News Bulletin", when my father used to sit glued to the radio listening for the reports on the success or failure of the sealing fleet. Little did I think in those far-off days that one day the S.S. *Eagle* would carry me to the ends of the earth.

The S.S. *Eagle* had been operated by Bowring Brothers under a succession of great sealing captains, and was one of the most successful ships in the sealing fleet. In fact she placed fourth in the ships bringing the most pelts home over her lifetime at the ice. In 1908, she had been rebuilt by a local shipwright, Mr. H.J. Taylor, who changed her bow to give her better ice-breaking capabilities.

In 1924, the S.S. *Eagle* was the first Newfoundland sealing ship to carry an aircraft for seal spotting. The plane was a baby Avro piloted by the legendary Newfoundland pilot, Captain Roy Grandy of Grand Bank. That year the *Eagle* was the first in and brought home a bumper load of pelts.

Now, as the last of the old, wooden-walled steamers, the S.S. *Eagle* still went to the seal hunt, but when that was over she spent most of her time tied up at Bowring's wharf on the Southside of St. John's. Occasionally there might be a call to open some local, ice-clogged port or a charter to bring a load of supplies to the United States' bases in Greenland, but these charters were few and far between. When she was lying up, Skipper Tom Carroll, who was now the Third Officer for the Antarctic trip, served as her caretaker. To Skipper Tom who had sailed as bo'sun for many a voyage to the ice, the old ship was home.

As I sat there alone in the saloon, I thought of the thousands of sealers who had gone to the ice in her, more than seven thousand men according to Skipper Tom, to face the dangers of the ice floes to make a few dollars to feed their families. I imagined I could hear their voices and the flurry of talk and stories as they collected their duffs from the steward's pantry. Maybe they would be first back from the ice and collect the coveted prize of pipe and tobacco this year, or maybe find a watery grave as so many sealers did among the treacherous northern ice floes.

My thoughts were interrupted by the entrance of another man. It turned out he was Jim Harding, the Steward. We introduced ourselves, and then he offered me a cup of tea, which I gratefully accepted.

At that time it was tradition on Newfoundland ships to always keep the kettle on the boil atop the galley stove. In fact the fire in the galley stove was never allowed to go out, and one of the chief duties of each watch was to make sure the fire was kept going.

I watched as Jim took a fistful of loose tea from the box under his pantry counter and threw it into a big teapot. Then, he went back to the galley, brought back the steaming kettle, filled the pot, and put the kettle on the saloon stove to keep it hot. In a few minutes I was sitting down to a good mug-up of scalding tea, round ships' biscuits and butter, and marmalade. It was the first of many meals I would eat in that historic saloon.

It was now 10:30 and mug-up time for the rest of the officers and crew. It was my first chance to meet my new shipmates and they certainly made me feel welcome.

The talk, of course, was about the great voyage to Antarctica. The word was that we were to leave St. John's about the third week in October, and go to North Sydney, Nova Scotia to take on board our main load of coal. This would be stowed in the lower deck of number two hatch. Later during the voyage, I found out that this was for bunkering at sea, as well as for the base camps to be set up in Antarctica. The main bunker of the *Eagle* could only carry ninety tons of coal, and as she was a real coal guzzler this was only enough to last four days. The coal in the lower deck would keep the main bunker supplied during our long sea voyage.

It was now October 12. In about a week we would be on our way, however, there was still a lot of work to be done before leaving St. John's.

After mug-up my shipmates went back to their work. I stepped outside the saloon and had the good fortune to meet Mr. Robert Whitten, the Second Officer. I introduced myself and before I could say another word he told me that two men were assigned to paint my cabin and the wireless room the next morning. I was very pleased to hear that my quarters were to be upgraded.

Just before noon Captain Sheppard came aboard and asked to speak with me after dinner. At exactly twelve o'clock, the steward came to the door of the saloon and rang a large school bell. Immediately all the officers went to wash up and then filed into their places. The table was set for ten, four on each side and one at either end. The meal was corned beef and cabbage with vegetables and a peas pudding, followed by a steamed raisin pudding, and, of course, cups and cups of scalding hot tea.

Chapter 4

There is always a good deal of curiosity among seamen when they meet their new shipmates and it was with great interest that I learned a little about the men I was to sail with on this great adventure.

Over dinner I found out a little more about Captain Sheppard who was fifty-five years old, and had started his career on the old square-riggers. He had earned a Foreign-going Master's ticket which allowed him to command any class of ship. The captain was well known and highly thought of by the British naval authorities for having convoyed confiscated Vichy-French ships across the Atlantic after the fall of France to the Germans. He was the St. John's Harbour Master when the British Admiralty asked him to command the S.S. *Eagle* to Antarctica.

Next to Captain Sheppard, in chain-of-command, was Captain Abe Butler. He, too, was a highly respected foreign-going captain and was our First Officer.

I had earlier met Robert Whitten, the Second Officer. He had had a lot of experience in the Arctic and had served on the famed Balbo-Labrador expedition.

Tom Carroll, the Third Officer, also had a lot of Arctic experience, and had served with Bartlett on the Perry expedition to the North Pole. Despite his eighty-one years, he was still a very powerful and active man who could shinny up to the crow's nest quicker than any other man on the ship. He had served so long on the *Eagle* that he seemed to be a part of the old ship.

The Chief Engineer, Charles Lewis, had served most of his life on ships operated by Bowring Brothers, and was one of the first marine engineers to earn a Chief Engineer's ticket in Newfoundland.

The Second Engineer was Frank Power, a veteran of coal-fired engines. He left the comforts and security of a large marine repair shop for the excitement and danger of a voyage to the bottom of the world.

The Third Engineer was Patrick Ring. Patrick was a long-time companion of Chief Engineer Lewis, and having made many voyages on the S.S. *Eagle*, he knew her engine from the boilers to the smokestack.

John Hayward had signed on as carpenter and bo'sun. As the S.S. *Eagle* was a wooden ship, the carpenter's job was a full-time one. He never went by his proper name but for some reason was always called "Chippie".

Patrick (Nick) Furlong, was the Chief Steward. James Harding was the Second Steward and I, Harold Squires, was the Wireless Officer and Purser. Later I would get to know the six deckhands and seamen, and eight firemen and oilers who with the first and second cooks made up our ship's company of twenty-eight men.

It was a good meal in good company, and when the other officers got up from the table to go back to work, Captain Sheppard motioned for me to stay. When they had all left the saloon, he gave me the opening I wanted by asking what my opinion was of the wireless equipment on board ship.

This was the chance I had hoped for, to bring my concerns to the attention of the ship's captain. I very carefully explained the transmitter's capabilities, both its frequency and its range. Captain Sheppard listened attentively while I spoke and then asked one question, "Was the wireless equipment presently on board the *Eagle* okay for a trip from St. John's to Cape Horn?"

My answer was that the onboard equipment was okay as long as we stayed in the major sea lanes. Captain Sheppard nodded his approval of my answer.

"Don't worry," Captain Sheppard reassured me, "when we get to the Falkland Islands they're going to install a whole new set of wireless equipment. It will be powerful enough to make contact with the British Isles from Antarctica."

I was relieved to hear this news, for I had feared that we might be expected to operate with the old short-range equipment which would have been useless in such an isolated area.

Then Captain Sheppard spoke to me of the dangers of our voyage. Besides the natural dangers of such a voyage the U-boats were still very active and the end of the war seemed far away. He also gave me our secret code name, "Tabarin", and told me that we would be joined in the Falkland Islands by the members of the British Expeditionary Antarctic force. The English party was to join us on the *Eagle* for the final leg of the voyage to Hope Bay. I was a bit surprised when Captain Sheppard added that we would also pick up twenty-five Labrador Husky dogs in the Falklands which had been taken there already. They would be the means of surface transportation during the expedition's stay in Antarctica.

Having laid my fears to rest about the wireless equipment, Captain Sheppard bid me good day, and I rose and went back to my work area. I was happy about the new equipment to be installed in the Falklands, it would make my job a little less difficult. I also felt better after having made the acquaintance of my fellow officers and shipmates. I was now impatient for our voyage to begin.

CHAPTER 5

At dinner the next day Captain Sheppard told us our tentative date of departure for Sydney, Nova Scotia was set for Tuesday morning, October 24, 1944. That gave us exactly one week to get everything in readiness to sail with a Halifax-bound convoy. It would be a busy week, for there were still a lot of supplies to be loaded and the renovations to the S.S. *Eagle* had to be completed.

I spent that last week checking out the ship's wireless equipment with the local Marconi Company. The storage batteries were recharged and I picked up a few necessary spare parts in case of an emergency at sea. The main wireless antenna was properly secured for the long sea voyage.

As well, Captain Sheppard had asked me to devise some means of getting a radio time signal to the bridge, so that he could keep the ship's chronometer accurate. It was important that the time signal be relayed to the bridge the instant it was received. I knew how important an accurate chronometer was for navigation, for it helped determine the ship's longitude. As the S.S. *Eagle* had been mainly used in the seal hunt and coastal trade, accurate time signals had not been important, therefore there was no connection from the wireless room to the chart room.

After some experimenting I solved the problem by rigging an electric push-bell from the wireless room, which was aft on the boat deck to Captain Sheppard's bedroom amidships, which served as the chart room. After I worked out a few little bugs, the system worked very well, and I could relay the time check with very little loss of time whenever Captain Sheppard needed it.

Living conditions on the S.S. *Eagle*, like most of the other old sealing ships of her class, were deplorable. As I have already said, the sanitary arrangements were still primitive and there was little that could be done to improve them. However, her owners, Bowring Brothers of St. John's did make some very necessary improvements for the Antarctic voyage.

The *Eagle*, because she had usually sailed north, had no refrigeration. The company now added a large ice box and later on the long voyage through the tropics it was worth its weight in gold. At each port of call we took on a fresh supply of ice and then filled our ice box with fresh food. It meant that we had fresh meat and vegetables for the entire voyage. But an ice box on the S.S. *Eagle*! Some of the old sealing captains would turn in their graves to think her officers and crew had grown so soft. Pork and duff was good enough fare for any self-respecting sailor.

During that first week there was one incident I shall never forget—our first lifeboat drill. When Captain Sheppard, schooled in the traditions of the British Navy, decided to have a lifeboat drill before putting to sea, old Skipper Tom Carroll scratched his head and said he couldn't remember the last time the *Eagle's* lifeboats had been lowered from the davits. In fact, he couldn't remember them ever being lowered at all during the years he had served on her.

He proved to be right, for when the crew attempted to lower the boats, they were frozen solid in the davits and nothing could budge them. We pushed and pulled and hauled, but nothing moved. It took Chippie, and all the crew working full out before they gave up the fight, and to a great cheer from the officers and men finally the lifeboat went over the side. Needless to say Captain Sheppard made sure they were in tip-top working condition before we sailed. On our next lifeboat drill the boats dropped from the davits without any trouble, and our lifeboat drill was a grand success. For the rest of the voyage, Captain Sheppard made sure the lifeboats were in readiness for immediate launch. Following that first harrowing lifeboat drill experience we were all issued Lifeboat Drill Certificates.

The day before we were due to depart, several boxes of small pine trees were delivered to the S.S. *Eagle*. They were a gift from the Newfoundland Government to Sir Alan Crandall, then Governor of the Falkland Islands. These pines, if they survived the rigours of the voyage, were to be planted on the grounds of the Falkland Islands' Government House. Captain Sheppard took the plants on board, and appointed a crewmember to look after them. On the long voyage to the Falklands, it would be no easy task to keep those northern seedlings alive. However, they survived the voyage and were turned over to Sir Alan in a proper ceremony on our safe arrival in Port Stanley in the Falklands.

The week slipped quickly away and there was a thousand last things to do or get before we went out through the Narrows. But at last, as far as we could tell, everything was ready for the grand voyage to Antarctica. So, on Monday, October 23, 1944, Captain Sheppard told us we would be sailing the following morning with a Halifax-bound convoy.

I met Captain Sheppard as I was returning from a shore visit, and Captain Sheppard asked me to accompany him to a convoy conference that afternoon to receive our sailing orders. As it was still wartime, "and the enemy might be listening", all sailing orders were given at the last moment and the press was silent about shipping movements.

It was interesting to listen to the Convoy Captain lay down our sailing orders and what we would do in case of an enemy attack. He told us that in the morning when we started to get under way, each ship in the convoy would be assigned a convoy position and he told us to try and maintain that position at all costs. Then he rose and wished us all good day. We left to go back on board the *Eagle*.

In the cool, grey dawn of Tuesday, October 24, we got ready to take up our convoy position. I was in the wireless shack when Captain Sheppard sent for me to go to the bridge. As soon as I stepped outside on the deck I knew the reason for my summons for a naval corvette was coming towards the *Eagle* with her Aldis lamp flashing.

As soon as I reached the bridge, Captain Sheppard asked me to reply to the corvette's signal. I flashed the letter "K" with our lamp, which was the code word for "Transmit your message, we are ready to receive."

I then took down the following message: "You are to take up your sailing position as the last ship in column number one and I will follow you out through the Narrows."

I passed on the message to Captain Sheppard who told me to reply: "Message received, we will follow your instructions."

The corvette then returned to her station and we cast off our lines in preparation to join the other ships slowly steaming out to sea. As we steamed towards the Narrows through the mass of wartime shipping that crowded the land-locked harbour, they blew their whistles as a farewell gesture for in those dangerous times no one knew who would be coming back.

Then, as we passed the lighthouse at Fort Amherst, where Captain Sheppard had once served as lighthouse keeper, the present keeper saluted us with a few blasts on the fog horn, which sounded strange on a fogless morning. This parting gesture drew a few smiles from the ship's company, but still it made us feel just a little bit more important. We replied with the blast of our steam whistle that echoed from the surrounding hills.

Outside the shelter of the harbour, the old S.S. *Eagle* began to dip into the rolling North Atlantic waves, as she had done for the past forty-one years on her annual voyage to the northern ice floes. Now, she was about to pit her strength against the southern ice mass of Antarctica.

As the Newfoundland coast faded into the distance, we all realized this was the moment we had been waiting for, the great adventure had truly begun, with our first leg of the journey being to Sydney, Nova Scotia where we would take on a supply of coal.

In convoy to Sydney, Nova Scotia

Once at sea, it didn't take long to settle down to the regular routine of sailing in convoy and we proceeded on our way without alarms or attacks. We kept radio silence except for any changes in our sailing position for fear of alerting any enemy submarines that might be prowling about and I busied myself with making everything shipshape in the wireless shack.

Towards nightfall, Captain Sheppard dropped into my cabin to see if I could get an up-to-date weather forecast for him. He told me the "glass" was falling and he thought we might be in for a bit of a blow.

He also asked if I minded being called to the bridge on short notice during the night, as he might need me to receive or send some message to the corvette or the other ships in our convoy. He then explained that neither he, nor the other ship's officers, although they knew the Morse Code, felt competent enough to send and receive messages.

I assured him I would be only too happy to help in any way I could. He thanked me for my co-operation, and then as he was leaving, turned, and said with a little smile, "Well Sparks, I guess tonight the old girl will show us what she's like in wind and rough seas if that storm that's brewing hits us." He closed the door to the wireless shack and went back to the bridge.

I immediately got down to work and searched the air waves for a weather forecast for our area. Captain Sheppard was right, we were in for a real blow. I went up to the bridge and passed on the forecast. Captain Sheppard shook his head, "It's going to be rough, Sparks," he said. "Make sure that everything that can move is fastened down, I expect she'll do some fancy dancing before this is over."

It wasn't long before the storm had hit us. The old ship began to creek and groan under the onslaught of wind and waves. As the wind increased she dipped her prow deeper into the waves, and began to roll a little. I got up and fas-

Rough sea

tened my cabin door open so that I could see the bridge. While I waited, I tried again for a new weather forecast. Then, Mr. Whitten, the Second Mate came out on the bridge and waved his arms. This was the agreed signal for me to proceed to the bridge. I pulled on my duffle coat, fastened the wireless shack door shut and went on up to the bridge.

The naval corvette was steaming towards us, and she circled around our stern, and then came back flashing the following message: "Winds increasing, bad weather ahead, try and maintain present speed and remain in convoy position."

I relayed the message to Captain Sheppard. He told me to acknowledge the message, and say we would follow instructions to the best of our ability. On receipt of our acknowledgement the corvette steamed back to the head of the convoy.

As we stood on the bridge watching her cut through the waves, Captain Sheppard spoke to me about his main fear — the *Eagle* in a really bad storm.

"Sparks," he said, "the *Eagle* is pretty much like the old S.S.*Terra Nova* was. A splendid ship in ice, in fact the *Terra Nova* was so good in ice, Captain Scott and his crew nicknamed her the "Terra Push" when she took them on their last ill-fated voyage to Antarctica. But in the open seas in rough weather, she rolled something awful, sometimes as much as fifty degrees. She was a coal guzzler too, just like the *Eagle*, and had to carry a tremendous amount of coal below decks. The danger was always that on one of those rolls the coal below decks would shift, and then she wouldn't be able to right herself. On one occasion, the *Terra Nova* rolled so far over that the lee coamings on her hatches were in the water. That time she righted herself and kept on going. Now, Sparks, I think that's what happened to the old *Terra Nova* on that voyage back from Greenland in 1943. She rolled so far over, the coal choked off her bilge pumps, and down she went. Anyway, if this storm keeps up we'll test out the *Eagle* tonight."

With the thought that the *Eagle* might suffer the fate of the *Terra Nova*, I made my way back to the wireless shack. It wasn't easy going, for while I was on the bridge the storm had intensified and the wind was howling in the rigging. The old *Eagle* was making mad plunges into the sea, and then staggering like a drunken sailor. There was no doubt that Captain Sheppard was right. After tonight, if we survived, we would all know the capabilities of the old girl. Slowly, and holding on for dear life, I made it back to the wireless shack and prepared to wait out the storm.

Chapter 6

That first night at sea was a sailor's nightmare. The waves became mountainous, and the old ship pitched, rolled and wallowed in wild abandonment. Unlike the larger iron ships I had sailed on, the hurricane force winds made the rigging of the *Eagle* howl and shriek like a human soul lost in eternal torments. As she rolled, I gave myself up for lost and prepared to meet my Maker. Each minute I figured was our last before she foundered and dipped beneath the waves forever. But I was wrong, she took the gale in full force and we were still afloat when morning came and the winds abated.

Twice during the night I was called to the bridge to read signals from other ships in the convoy. During my last trip to the bridge, Captain Sheppard wondered how the naval escort was making out in such a gale. She was, Captain Sheppard said, a British built corvette of what was known in naval circles as the "Flower Class". They were called this because each corvette was named for an English flower. These ships were built to ride high in the water. This gave them greater speed and ability to manoeuvre in their pursuit of enemy submarines. Captain Sheppard thought these corvettes would, like the *Eagle*, have a pretty rough time of it in weather such as we had experienced during the night.

The storm blew itself out just before dawn and with daybreak we discovered that during the night we had fallen far behind the convoy and were now alone, a sitting duck for any enemy submarine that might be lurking in the area. I was on the bridge just after daybreak, and I thought that Captain Sheppard, who had stayed on watch all night, looked very tired and haggard in the cold, grey light of early dawn.

"Well, Sparks," he said to me, "we're all alone, and we still have a full day's steam to Sydney. Make sure you have our exact position at all times, in case we have to send out an SOS message. But," he added on a more cheerful note, "the glass is rising."

Nothing out of the ordinary happened and we made it into Sydney harbour without incident. Our voyage to Sydney from St. John's had taken three days and two hours.

At this time, although a sister British Dominion, Canada was a foreign country and we had to identify ourselves to enter the port. When we were given permission to enter Sydney harbour a pilot came on board and we were told to dock at Witney Pier. Here we would load our coal for the trip south and once again we had to produce our papers before being allowed to dock.

As every sailor who has ever sailed on a coal-burner knows, the coal dust makes everything unbelievably dirty. However, it had to be done, and in just two hours we had loaded our coal. Then, without a proper shore leave in Sydney, we were off to join another convoy bound for Halifax. For the rest of this part of the voyage, the *Eagle's* crew fell to with a will to try and clean away the coal dust from the decks and hatches by using a powerful water nozzle with heavy jets of ocean water. It took many hours of hard labour, but before we reached Halifax they had managed to get rid of most of the coal dust on the deck.

We arrived safely in Halifax on the evening of October 28, 1944, after a voyage of thirty-nine hours from our departure out of Sydney. Our stay at Halifax was supposed to be for one week in order to have a new generator installed to expand the capacity of the *Eagle's* rather limited electrical system.

During our stay in Halifax, I asked Captain Sheppard to arrange for a new wireless antenna to be installed. This would increase our wireless range considerably. It was a busy week for all the *Eagle's* crew for Captain Sheppard had a number of things he wanted done before we started on the second leg of our voyage, which was to the West Indies. Of course, there was shore leave, which all hands enjoyed, for Halifax at that time was a sailor's city.

The storm on our voyage from St. John's to Sydney had given Captain Sheppard a good idea of the limitations of the *Eagle* in rough seas, so he sat down with the Halifax Naval Authorities to plot the best course from Halifax to Port Stanley in the Falkland Islands. He was pleased with their assistance and felt we would have a safe voyage.

All of us had been made aware of how important it was that we get to Antarctica before their winter season set in. The Antarctic summer being short, and once ended, the *Eagle* would not be able to operate in the ice conditions that would then prevail. The deadline for the establishment of the land base at Hope Bay was the end of March. We would have to be out of there by then or be frozen-up for the winter season. Because of this urgency, everything connected with the *Eagle* was a rush job and the naval authorities at Halifax made sure that the work on the generator was finished on time.

On November 7 we said farewell to Halifax and started off again. Once outside the port of Halifax, Captain Sheppard set his course for Bermuda, where we would take on fresh supplies. This time we had no surface escorts but were promised air surveillance along the way.

On our second day at sea we hit the warm waters of the Gulf Stream. It began to grow hot, and we made a most unpleasant discovery. As the heat increased, the deck of the *Eagle* began to blister and great bubbles of pitch and some other smelly substance appeared all along the deck planks. The odour was sickening. I didn't know what was causing it until Skipper Tom Carroll explained it to me.

"You see, Markie, me son, this old ship has been to the seal hunt for forty-two seasons and brought home her share of seal pelts. Now most seasons, she had a deck-load as well as being filled below and the seal blubber got into the pitch. When 'tis cold it don't matter. Now, with all the heat it's come alive again."

Rotted seal blubber! Well that explained it but it was the most ungodly stench I'd ever encountered in my life. As we steamed further south, the stench became stronger and the decks became so slippery that it became almost impossible to walk on them. As well, we got the blubber pitch on our shoes and clothing. Its noxious odour filled the ship making it impossible to escape the overpowering smell.

We arrived in Bermuda on November 10, and Captain Sheppard's first order was to get some rough planks and nail them over the main deck, making a board walk, so that we could at least move about again. There was nothing that could be done about the stinking blubber pitch, except to hope we made a quick passage to the cooler waters of the Falkland Islands.

We all enjoyed our two-day stay in Bermuda and for a short time at least could get away from the odour of boiling seal blubber. On November 12 we raised our anchor and set out for Trinidad. This would be a nine-day voyage for the *Eagle*, which meant that the crew would have to bunker coal at sea. This involved taking coal from the lower decks of the ship to the bunker room near the engine.

Bunkering coal in the tropics.

When the steering chain under my cabin floor became very active I went to the bridge to investigate and found Mr. Butler, our First Officer, at the helm. He explained about the bunkering, and then, as all the crew were involved in this activity asked me if I would like to try a trick at the helm.

I was only too happy to have a go at the wheel and after rigging a small loud speaker from the wireless room to the bridge so as not to miss any transmission, I took over. Mr. Butler, although he was anxious to supervise the bunkering, kindly stayed on the bridge for a few moments until I got the hang of it. I really enjoyed my turn at the wheel, as it was my first experience of handling a ship at sea.

Nine days, six hours out of Bermuda we made port at Trinidad. Here we took on new supplies, including more coal for the voyage down the coast of South America, and a cargo of a very different nature.

It was on our second day in Trinidad that Captain Sheppard called me to his cabin. "I've a little job for you, Sparks," he said. "I want you to go and see how many of the officers and crew are interested in buying a case of rum at 75 cents a bottle. You can write down the names and I'll have the money deducted from their pay."

My face must have registered my surprise at this strange request, for I immediately had visions of a drunken ship's crew running madly around the old ship. Captain Sheppard hastened to allay my fears.

"Don't worry Sparks," he said with a grin, "I'll keep control of the rum and issue it at my discretion. They need something to overcome that stench of blubber."

"Aye, aye, Sir," I said, and went off with a pad and pencil on what might be considered a mission of mercy. I started with the officers, and got a quick "yes" to my question. They agreed the rum should be controlled by the captain. One or two wanted two cases, but Captain Sheppard had limited each person to one case.

I caught up with old Skipper Tom Carroll on the aft deck. He had seen me writing down names and asked what I was up to. "The Captain wants to know if you'd like to buy a 12 bottle case of rum at 75 cents a bottle?" I explained.

Skipper Tom looked at me, shook his head, wiped the sweat from his face and sat down on a nearby hatch. He looked at me again, and then said, "Markie, ask me that question again me son. I don't think I heard you right the first time."

"I asked you if you wanted to buy a 12-bottle case of rum at 75 cents a bottle."

He jumped to his feet, wiped his brow again. "That's what I thought you said, me son, but couldn't believe it. Of course, I'll have a case of rum, Markie, two, if I can get 'em. It's the bit of grog what keeps me going b'y," and with a broad smile of anticipation he put his hat back on and continued aft.

From Skipper Tom, I went to see, Mr. Lewis, the First Engineer. His concern was for the safety of his oilers and firemen. However, as soon as he knew the captain would control the liquor he said he wanted a case, but assured me for medicinal reasons only. I am happy to say Captain Sheppard controlled the rum and not once during our long voyage south were there any problems.

We left Trinidad on November 12, outward bound to Para, a small Brazilian seaport at the mouth of the Amazon River. We arrived there without incident on December 8, 1944.

From Para, we sailed for the port of Recife, formerly known as Pernambuco and arrived there on December 16. It was on this voyage we suffered our first injury. One of the firemen injured his hand in the stoke hold. He had to be left under medical care in Recife. This left us one hand short in the firemen's watch. However, one of the steward's helpers volunteered to go as a fireman and this evened up the firemen's watch again. We sailed from Recife on December 23 bound for the great seaport city of Rio de Janeiro.

We spent Christmas at sea in temperatures of 100°F, with the stench of our blistering decks more pungent than ever. Under these conditions it was a Christmas different from any we had known in Newfoundland. We marked the day with a special meal including a figgy duff, but as old salts most of us were used to spending Christmas at sea, and as we were at sea, there were no extra rum rations served.

We entered Rio de Janeiro in the same 100°F temperatures. What a sight to behold, with its sprawling white sandy beaches and the magnificent statue of Christ The Redeemer standing high on a mountain top overlooking the harbour.

Chapter 7

After we had docked in Rio on December 28, the port authorities notified the various Rio seamen's institutes of our arrival and thanks to these good people, we were able to enjoy a little of the Christmas celebrations.

Our first reminder of the festive season was the arrival of a "Christmas ditty bag" for each member of the ship's company, officers and crew alike. These ditty bags were put together by the good women of the seaport towns and distributed by the seamen's institutes. They contained such things as soap, shaving gear, writing paper, pens, pencils, nail files and a lot of other small, but very useful articles of everyday use. Accompanying the ditty bags was an invitation for all of us to celebrate Christmas with a turkey dinner at one of the neighbouring seamen's institutes.

The thought of a real turkey dinner did us all a world of good. We were now a little more than two months out of St. John's on our voyage to Antarctica and needless to say, with the stench of the bubbling pitch and seal blubber, it hadn't been a picnic for either the officers or the crew. As well, the S.S. *Eagle* had never been designed for service in the tropics. We soon discovered after we put to sea, that despite the work done to strengthen the old ship in the St. John's dockyard, she was still weak amidships. Another problem was that the water which gathered on the bridge dripped down into the main saloon beneath. In every port we had visited, the ship had to have repairs. This slowed us down so much that by the time we had reached Rio we were running well behind schedule.

However, now was the time to put all our troubles aside and enjoy the Christmas hospitality of the Rio seamen's institutes and this we resolved to do. Even old Skipper Tom Carroll got into the festive spirit. He came to my cabin, his powerful frame nearly filling it, and asked a favour. Would I trim his hair for the party? I immediately agreed, and he brought a chair from his cabin, put it on the deck, sat down, and was ready for action.

I was no professional barber, but did what I could with scissors and comb. While I was busy cutting his hair he told me a little about himself. He was eighty-one years old, but hale and hardy, having hardly known a day of sickness in his life. He had been working for Bowring Brothers of St. John's for over sixty years, and hoped to give them many more years of service. He had made countless voyages to the seal hunt off the Newfoundland coast and had been a member of the crew of the ship that landed Admiral Perry in the Arctic on his successful voyage to the North Pole.

My reputation as a barber soon spread, and shortly after Skipper Tom left, our other near octogenarian, Mr. Lewis, the Chief Engineer arrived with a similar request. I trimmed his hair and his fine white moustache as well.

Like Skipper Tom, Chief Lewis had grown old in the service of Bowring Brothers, and no mother ever tended her children more carefully than he tended the *Eagle's* engine. His regard and knowledge of what the engine could do led to a good-natured little war between he and the captain. Captain Sheppard was always looking for more speed, but Mr. Lewis claimed he was under orders from the owners to treat the engine very carefully. It was some months later we learned why he could never exceed a certain speed.

Chief Lewis thanked me for my help and said he was really looking forward to a good meal. He told me that as everyone, except for a small duty watch, was going ashore he intended to shut down the *Eagle* before he went ashore for the turkey dinner.

When he told Captain Sheppard his plans, the captain nodded his agreement. It was only when Chief Lewis was on his way to the dinner that Captain Sheppard realized what he meant by "shutting down".

Shutting down was an old sealing term, and when the ships were caught in the ice, the engines and generators were shut off to preserve the fuel supply. The sealing ships then reverted to using kerosene lamps. The *Eagle* was still fitted with kerosene lamps, and this was all that the duty watch would have until the next day when Chief Lewis started up the engine again. Captain Sheppard was staying on board with the duty watch and he had intended to catch up with his paper work. Now, too late he discovered what the chief had meant.

I was still on board ship, so Captain Sheppard asked if I would go to Frank Power, the Second Engineer, who was a member of the duty watch, and ask him to start the generator. I met up with Frank on the stairs leading to the bridge, and relayed the captain's request. He assured me that he was certainly willing to start the generator, but he had orders from the chief not to and he wouldn't dare disobey him. However, to help out the captain, he suggested setting up a light using one of my twelve volt batteries from the wireless room. This I thought was an excellent idea, and in a short while we had rigged a wire to Captain Sheppard's reading light.

The Christmas party was an event to be remembered and we all enjoyed ourselves immensely. The officers and crew of the S.S. *Eagle* conducted themselves splendidly. There wasn't one incident to mar the evening's festivities. The ship's crew were, without exception, a credit to their native land. We all made it back safely to our ship and the memories of that wonderful evening in Rio remained with us long after we said good-bye to that beautiful city.

On December 30 we got underway for our next port of call, the city of Montevideo in Uruguay. I was on the bridge during the ten mile voyage down the harbour of Rio in order to read any messages that might be flashed from the shore. It was a beautiful trip with the sharp outline of the white granite mountains towering some twenty-three hundred feet above us.

During the trip down Rio harbour to the sea, Captain Sheppard wanted to know how the party had gone. I was very pleased to tell him how successful it had been and of the excellent conduct of our crew. We then talked about the voyage and how hot it had become once we'd entered the tropics. Captain Sheppard then pointed at the bundles of clothing that were being dragged behind in the *Eagle's* wake.

"I made them haul off the old long johns," he said, "and they look like they're getting a good wash. They'll need them again soon, once we get a bit further south."

I didn't disagree with Captain Sheppard, but with the tropical sun pouring down from a blue, cloudless sky, and the temperature showing 100°F, I didn't really think we'd need long johns again for quite some time. There were several other discomforts the crew suffered on our voyage down the coast of Brazil. One was the tepid water we had to drink, and the other was that the crew had to double up in the bunks, and to get out of the top bunks they had to step on the mess table to get to the floor. And always there was the stink of seal blubber filling their nostrils. But despite all the difficulties they went about their work and complained very little.

Three days out of Rio, Captain Sheppard told us that Mr. Butler, our First Officer, was ill and on arrival in Montevideo he would have to enter hospital for treatment of a hernia. After the surgery he was to be sent back to St. John's to recover.

This was a very serious disappointment for Captain Sheppard. Mr. Butler was an excellent navigator and the captain's right-hand man where navigation was concerned.

The ship's bunkers were running low on coal, so it was time to bunker at sea again. This meant that while the crew was busy transferring the coal from below deck to the bunkers, I would take over the steering duties. It would be strange to be there without Mr. Butler who always took his position on the bridge while the coal was being shovelled. However, everything went well, and we entered the River Plate, took on a pilot, and headed up river for Montevideo.

A little way up the River Plate, our pilot pointed out the wreckage of the famous German pocket battleship, *Graf Spee*, which had been scuttled by her commander after a sharp fight with H.M.S. *Exeter*, *Ajax* and *Achilles* on December 13, 1939. Part of *Graf Spee's* superstructure and some gun turrets could still be seen. We passed very close to the wreck on our way up river and it was a powerful reminder of the war that was still raging.

CHAPTER 8

On January 6, 1945, we arrived in Montevideo. We were met at dockside by our ship's agents, the well-known firm of McLean & Stapleton. This firm had acted as agents to many Antarctic explorers over the years.

We had been expecting that on our arrival in Montevideo we would meet up with the ship bringing the English members of the expedition, as well as the Labrador Husky dogs that were to accompany them. However, our agents told Captain Sheppard that the English ship had arrived earlier and both the expedition members and the dogs had been transferred to the S.S. *Fitzroy*, a cargo ship that sailed between Montevideo and Port Stanley in the Falkland Islands. They had left on Christmas Eve and we would meet up with them at Port Stanley for the final leg of the journey.

The dogs that had been chosen to go on the expedition had been culled from the best dog teams on the Labrador coast. Earlier in the year an expedition member had gone to Labrador, and with the help of a Newfoundland Ranger, had scoured the Labrador coast for the best dogs available. The dogs had then been taken to St. John's in an old Customs' cutter and shipped to England on another ship. In Liverpool,

England, they had been transferred onboard the ship carrying the English expedition members to Montevideo.

Captain Sheppard informed the ship's agents about Mr. Butler's illness and a doctor was at once sent on board. He confirmed that Mr. Butler was suffering from a strangulated hernia and made the necessary arrangements for him to enter a local hospital. We all visited him, wished him luck during his hospital stay, and a speedy safe return voyage home.

His absence required Captain Sheppard to appoint someone to take over as first officer. He promoted Mr. Whitten to First Officer, Skipper Tom Carroll became Second Mate, and John Hayward, carpenter and bo'sun moved up to Third Mate.

As our ship's company was now reduced in number, the watches had to be divided into six hours on and six hours off, instead of the former eight hours on and eight off. Needless to say Mr. Whitten and Skipper Tom took their new duties in stride and everything went along as smoothly as before. The only thing was that Captain Sheppard, being the only navigator on the ship, had his workload increased.

We spent several days in Montevideo preparing for our run to Port Stanley, our point of departure for Antarctica. Then, to our great delight on Saturday our ship's agents informed us that on Sunday, a Montevideo inn, an allied seamen's institute, would be sponsoring an outing for the crews of all the Allied ships in port.

A bus would pick us up early Sunday morning and take us to a place where there would be swimming in a pond. This was very welcome news to the crew of the *Eagle*, for as we had no showers or baths on board ship, getting a body wash wasn't easy. What we had to do was find a secluded place on the ship, strip, then haul up a bucket of sea water and douse it over ourselves. Now, we really looked forward to getting a good wash in fresh water, as well as having a good time. When we boarded the bus each man had his "cake" of soap ready, and between the smell of the blistering deck and the tropical heat we needed lots of soap and water.

The outing was a grand success, and after the swimming a barrel of beer was rolled out and glass mugs, sandwiches and cakes were provided. We were like kids at the circus. Everything was provided free-of-charge by the Liberty Inn and served by the women of the Allied Services Club.

The Liberty Inn, under British management, treated us as full members, and we were invited to make the Inn our social headquarters during our stay. The Inn, a friendly place with lots of atmosphere, had a large fireplace in the main lounge where a good fire blazed away to cheer the heart of a homesick sailor. There was a piano which got lots of use and many a good singsong was held around it. There were also several billiard rooms, and it was a wonderful place to meet with other Allied sailors. As well, the British Patriotic Committee of Montevideo published a small pamphlet entitled, "A Sailor's Guide to Montevideo", which was invaluable in finding your way around the city as it listed hotels, churches, clubs and stores where English was spoken.

Forty-six years later I still have my copy of "A Sailor's Guide to Montevideo". Whenever I look at it, it brings back very happy memories of the Liberty Inn and the good fellowship it provided for sailors of all the different countries that made up the Allied Navy.

However, all good things come to an end, and on January 10, 1945, we said good-bye to Montevideo and the Liberty Inn, and set sail for Port Stanley in the Falklands.

We were not too long at sea when it became apparent that we were leaving the warmer climate behind. The air started to grow colder and the discarded long johns once again came into their own. We now began to come into contact with the large birds of the southern seas—the albatross and the Cape pigeons.

The weather soon became more like that of home. The Falkland Islands lie in the same latitude as Newfoundland, only Newfoundland is north of the equator, and the Falklands lie south. It was now summer in the Falklands. In 1944, the two islands had other similarities—they were both crown colonies, ruled by a British governor appointed from London.

We were looking forward to getting to the Falkland Islands as it would be the first English-speaking country since leaving Halifax. The currency in the Falklands was the British pounds, shillings and pence. Port Stanley was also our last stop before taking on the dangers of Antarctica.

As it was a seven-day voyage to Port Stanley from Montevideo, we had one more coal passing to bunker the *Eagle*. We needed a very calm day and we all hoped it would be the last coal passing on the outward voyage. Everything went well and the coal passing was over, for a time anyway.

A few days before we arrived at the Falklands, I borrowed a book from Captain Sheppard and read-up on the Islands. I was amazed to learn that there were over two hundred islands in the Falkland group, and Port Stanley was the capital.

The Falklands lie about two hundred and fifty miles east of the coast of Argentina. That country has always laid claim to them, but they had remained under British rule. However, the Argentinian government was trying to establish its authority in the area.

The islands were bare of trees, the fierce gales of wind in the area preventing their growth. When I read this, I knew why we had brought the pine seedlings from Newfoundland as a gift to the Governor. These hardy trees of a similar climate might just take root and grow there. The only vegetation on the islands was the giant tussock grass. It grew all over the islands, usually in tall clumps, sometimes reaching a height of six feet.

In 1945, the economic life of the Falklands was dependent on wool and the island was divided into large sheep ranches which provided employment for many people. The distance between ranches was considerable and could only be covered by horse or boat. There were no roads except in the vicinity of Port Stanley.

There was also a large trading company called the Falkland Islands Dependencies. It operated two ships as well as general stores with the main store in Port Stanley. There were also a number of government and community jobs, as in every small British colony.

The main source of domestic fuel in the Falklands was peat. The people of the islands had to cut, store, dry and cart the peat to their own localities for winter's fuel. Very little coal was used for fuel or cooking purposes on the islands.

As I was reading the description of the islands, I was suddenly brought back to the *Eagle* by a loud shout from Captain Sheppard who was on the bridge. He was telling the men on watch that the first person to sight the Falklands would receive a bottle of rum. This made everybody strain their eyes, for we knew we must be nearing land.

A few minutes later a cry of "Land Ho!" went up from Able Seaman Tom Kelly and we all rushed to peer in the direction he was pointing. First, we could see nothing but after a little while we saw the first grey outlines of the Falklands rising out of the ocean.

Captain Sheppard kept his word, and Mr. Kelly was presented with his prize. When his watch was finished, he and the other members of the watch went below and made short work of the contents of the bottle.

As we neared Port Stanley, the *Cleo*, the Harbour Master's steam launch met us and we took on a pilot. He was an old master mariner, a friendly soul who pointed out a number of old ships anchored in the harbour. One was the old coal hulk, *Phennia*, a former three-thousand-ton, full-rigged ship that had plied for many years the Australian trade. She had been condemned at Port Stanley after being dismasted while rounding Cape Horn. Other old ships anchored were also victims of the Horn and having found refuge at Port Stanley, remained there.

Docked in Port Stanley in the Falkland Islands.

We docked at last and were eagerly looking forward to our shore leave in a sister British colony. Even though it was at the other end of the earth, they spoke English, and for the first time in three months we were able to understand everything being said without the aid of an interpreter. It wasn't home but it was the next best thing to being there.

CHAPTER 9

We enjoyed our stay in the Falkland Islands, but it was a very busy time. The first thing of course, as in every other port we had made on our long voyage south, was to make repairs to the S.S. *Eagle*. Because it was the last port of call before Antarctica, there were extensive repairs to put her in shipshape condition for the coming battle with the ice floes of that ice-bound continent.

The Falkland Islands' shipwrights took a great interest in the old ship, and realizing the importance of our getting to the Antarctic before the short summer season ended, they set to, and worked with a will. The old ship was recaulked and steel ties were placed amidships to strengthen her in what had proven to be her weakest part.

While the shipwrights were busy with their repairs, we were engaged in loading supplies for the journey to Hope Bay, the proposed site of the expedition's base camp. Hope Bay is on the northern tip of Antarctica.

We were all aware of the dangers and difficulties of our mission. The previous year, the S.S. *Fitzroy* in company with H.M.S. *William Scoresby* had tried in vain to navigate the ice-packed waters. They had failed to enter Hope Bay, and it was only after cruising along the coast of Graham Land that they had finally been able to establish a base at Port Lockroy. It was now the turn of the last of the famous, old wooden-walled Newfoundland sealing steamers to show her mettle, and push her way through the heavy ice where the steel-plated *Fitzroy* had failed, and enable the members of the expedition to set up a base camp at Hope Bay.

H.M.S. *William Scoresby*, built in 1927, had spent the war as a minesweeper and had also served to bring patients from the outlying islands to the hospital at Port Stanley. The *Scoresby* along with the *Fitzroy* were to accompany us as far as the former old whaling station at Deception Island in the South Shetland Islands. From there the S.S. *Eagle* would go it alone.

It was on this last stage of our long journey that we began to find out some of the details of our top secret mission. Our main job we knew was to help the British expedition get into Hope Bay and validate the British claim to that area. Antarctica was now considered of strategic importance because of the political situation in Argentina. The British government felt very strongly that Argentina should not at this time control the southern side of Drake Passage. In order to strengthen the British hand in the area, a small military force was, therefore, assembled under the British Admiralty. This force was known as Operation "Tabarin", Tabarin being the name of a well-known nightclub of that day. It was a suitable name for a group who had to spend many months in the darkness of an Antarctic winter.

The Admiralty wanted two British bases established in Antarctica, one at Deception Island, and the other at Hope Bay, the northern part of Graham Land. Deception Island had an excellent harbour, and according to members of the British expedition, enemy raiders had used its harbour as a base of operation earlier in the war. Now, the Admiralty would be able to monitor any enemy activity in the area, as well as neutral ships who might come that way.

Captain Robert Sheppard (left) and
Commander Jimmy (Scout) Marr (right)

Operation "Tabarin" was under the command of Lieutenant (now) Commander Jimmy (Scout) Marr, who had earlier served as a member of the Shackleton Expedition. Marr had worked as a biologist in both the Arctic and Antarctic on a number of scientific expeditions and had been serving in the east on a minesweeper when he was put in charge of Operation "Tabarin". He had been on board the *Fitzroy* during the attempt to enter Hope Bay the previous year. Now, he intended to sail with us on the *Eagle*. He was given a tiny cabin aft that had been used in sealing days as a combined hospital-dispensary. It had been used as sleeping quarters by Mr. Butler our First Officer, until he'd been hospitalized in Montevideo. The little cabin had four bunks and a stove. It wasn't the most convenient cabin, for now our decks were laden with cargo and you had to scramble over the deck cargo to get to the dining saloon.

Commander Marr was a very pleasant Scot, who not only played the mouth organ, but had first-hand stories of his previous experiences in Antarctica. He soon became a great friend to the whole ship's company, especially to Captain Sheppard and myself.

David James, a serving naval officer, had earlier been appointed as assistant surveyor to the Falkland Islands Dependencies Survey and had come from England just a week before our arrival, to travel to Hope Bay on the *Eagle*.

Our departure date for Deception Island was now set for January 25. At this point Captain Sheppard advised the crew that the expedition would not provide the warm overcoats, sweaters and heavy trousers needed to survive in Antarctica. However, this proved to be no problem for the good people of Port Stanley, especially the local church groups who supplied all of our needs.

The S.S. *Eagle* was now so laden with cargo that it was decided the Labrador Huskies would remain on board the *Fitzroy*, as we did not have room for their pens. In fact we had so much cargo on our decks that it was difficult to get from one part of the ship to the other. This situation brought a chuckle from old Skipper Tom Carroll who was trying to get aft with How Curran, one of the crewmen. As he climbed over the piles of stores, he turned to How and said, "If they could only see us at "Mudges" now, How, what would they say?" "Mudges" was the old name for the Bowring Brothers premises on the Southside of St. John's Harbour, where the *Eagle* was usually berthed.

Yes, I thought, when I heard old Skipper Tom, what would they say back home if they could only see us. With every bit of deck space crammed with cargo, and an old scow on our quarterdeck to be used for transporting cargo on shore we were indeed a strange sight. But, we had one consolation. Thanks to the ten Port Stanley shipwrights, headed by Robert Reese, who had for ten days worked flat out, we were now seaworthy and ready to tackle Hope Bay.

CHAPTER 10

On Tuesday, January 23, 1945, the S.S. *Fitzroy* in company with H.M.S. *William Scoresby*, left Port Stanley for Deception Island. Both ships were heavily laden with supplies to be landed when the base camp was established. Captain Roberts of the Falkland Islands Dependencies Company, who was to share the responsibility of the expedition with Commander Marr, sailed on the *Fitzroy*. Commander Marr came with us on the S.S. *Eagle*.

We watched the *Fitzroy* and H.M.S. *William Scoresby* sail away, the *Fitzroy* towing a five-hundred-ton oil barge behind her. The oil barge was to be moored at Deception Island until the end of the summer season to supply the needs of the *William Scoresby*, the only oil-burning ship of the expedition. This meant the *William Scoresby* wouldn't have to return to the Falklands to refuel during the summer.

We had mixed feelings of anticipation and dread as we stood on the deck of the *Eagle* and watched the two ships fade into the twilight of the Southern hemisphere. In a day or two we would follow them, and only Heaven knew what dangers awaited us. All we knew was that it was not going to be an easy assignment.

We waited anxiously for January 24, the day set for our departure from Port Stanley. It was 746 miles to Deception Island, a four-day voyage if the weather was good. Deception Island was the last stop before we were to try to enter Hope Bay.

We left port on schedule and for the next few days had beautiful weather. This was important as a storm off Cape Horn might hold us up for days. In beautiful calm seas the old *Eagle* made a good seven knots, and everything progressed according to plan. A few days later Captain Sheppard again lent me the area description book that each ship carried. This book had an excellent description of the area where we were going. I read that the continent of Antarctica was larger than Europe and Australia combined and had no permanent inhabitants.

It is a vast continent, but only one percent of its surface is bare. The rest of the continent lies buried under a vast ice-cap ranging in depth from a few feet to two miles. Its area is approximately five million square miles.

This ice-cap has a cooling effect on the weather, as the air passing over Antarctica is lowered in temperature. Thus, the glacier-cap of Antarctica affects the weather of the southern part of the world. All around the continent the sea is frozen from May to October. However, during the short summer, the ice breaks up and moves about as a great field of floating icebergs. Although there are some sea mammals in the water around the continent, there are no native land animals.

January 26, 1945, dawned clear and with a fresh breeze from the northwest we were keeping good time. We were now about two hundred miles east of Cape Horn in the Drake Passage. Just after breakfast a cry of "Sail Ho!" went up from the man in the *Eagle's* crow's nest. I was in my cabin, but my door was open so I heard the cry, and rushed out on deck to see what ship was approaching. Able Seaman Alan

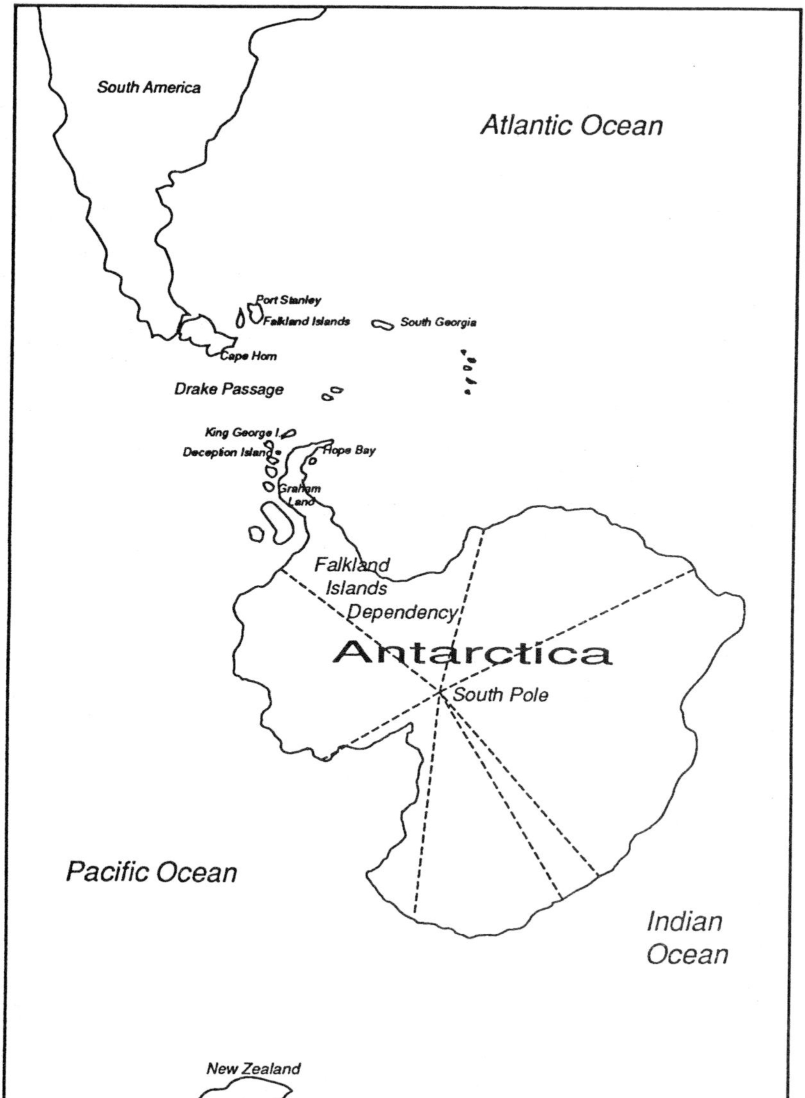
South America
Atlantic Ocean
Port Stanley
Falkland Islands
South Georgia
Cape Horn
Drake Passage
King George I.
Deception Island
Hope Bay
Graham Land
Falkland Islands Dependency
Antarctica
South Pole
Pacific Ocean
Indian Ocean
New Zealand

The barque Lawhill *in Drake Passage, January 26, 1945.*

Shano was at the wheel of the *Eagle* and he called asking the mate to tell Captain Sheppard that there was a sail on the horizon off our starboard bow.

Captain Sheppard came up on deck and soon identified the approaching vessel. He remarked that this would be a historic meeting, for the approaching ship, flying along under full sail, was the barque *Lawhill*, one of the last of two old four-masted, British "Cape Horners". Meeting her here, two hundred miles east in the Drake Passage was the S.S. *Eagle*, the last of the great, old wooden-walled Newfoundland sealing steamers. The *Eagle* from St. John's, Newfoundland, bound for Deception Island, and the *Lawhill* from Sydney, Australia, bound for Cape Town, South Africa.

The *Lawhill* was built in 1892, in Dundee, Scotland. She had a gross tonnage of 2,816 tons and measured 333 feet from stem to stern. Her owners were the Union Government of

South Africa. This beautiful towering sailing barque had successfully run the German submarine blockade in two wars and was still doing so in the early spring of 1945.

She was a thing of beauty as she passed within half a cable length of us on a parallel course, soon leaving us far behind. We saluted her with three blasts from our whistle, but she made no answer. Then, we parted company, and she soon disappeared over the horizon. It was a sight that none of us who were present at that historic moment would soon forget.

Seeing the *Lawhill* reminded Commander Marr of when he was with Shackleton in the *Nimrod* during Shackleton's 1922 voyage of exploration. They had met a great five-masted barque, the *France* in the same general area. History seemed to be repeating itself. We wondered what the crew of the *Lawhill* must have thought of us, the last of the old, wooden-walled steamers. We must have looked a motley sight with our decks crammed with boxes and bags of every description and one hundred and fifty carcasses of fresh mutton hanging from our rigging and spars. Then, to add to the confusion there was the old landing scow lashed to our deck.

The large number of mutton carcasses made up the main meat supply for the expedition, mutton being very plentiful and cheap in the Falkland Islands. The carcasses had been hung in the rigging to let them freeze, for the temperature was now dropping below freezing. As our Newfoundland fish supply was beginning to run out, it was comforting to know that we at least had mutton enough to supply our needs.

Up to this time the food served on the S.S. *Eagle* had followed the traditional pattern of meals served on Newfoundland ships. This consisted mainly of fish and brewis, home-baked beans, corned beef and cabbage and, of course, that traditional dish of the Newfoundland sealing ships, lop scouse. In fact we had lop scouse at least twice a week. This was a dish of boiled pork and vegetables, somewhere between a stew and a soup. As our supplies of Newfoundland fish ran out you would hear many a crewmember wishing for one last meal of fish.

By now we were getting closer to our rendezvous at Deception Island, before making our first attack on the ice at Hope Bay.

CHAPTER 11

During our stay at Port Stanley in the Falkland Islands, I had made a number of visits to the main wireless station operated by the British Navy. As a result of these visits, I got to know the wireless operators pretty well and struck up a number of lasting friendships. They were great fellows and went out of their way to help in any way they could. In fact, before we left Port Stanley, the wireless operators promised that whenever bad weather was forecast for the area of Deception Island and Hope Bay they would contact me.

This help was of crucial importance to us, for once we left Port Stanley we were entering a kind of no-man's land where the weather could change very suddenly and with very little warning. On January 27, as we neared the area of Deception Island, the first warning of an impending storm for our area was sent to me by the Port Stanley wireless operators.

I relayed the news of the threatening storm to Captain Sheppard and he was very worried. The *Eagle* on her way south had shown a great tendency to roll and pitch in heavy seas. Now, even more than before, we were laden with supplies and equipment for the expedition's base at Deception Island, and the proposed base at Hope Bay, if we succeeded in reaching there.

The forecast from my friends in Port Stanley came none too soon for the storm came on, and the waves driven by gale force winds were soon pounding against the old *Eagle*. She rolled and pitched, and the extra cargo made her very sluggish in the waves which slowed us down to about five knots. Captain Sheppard decided to stay on the bridge for the duration of the storm.

We were still observing the wartime rules of total blackout, and in the darkness of the gathering storm you could hardly see the other members of the watch. The blackout and the storm almost proved fatal to Captain Sheppard.

He had been on the bridge for quite a while before he decided to check something on the main deck. Just as he'd stepped on the ladder, the *Eagle* rolled and plunged violently forward. Captain Sheppard lost his footing and fell to the deck below. His cry for help was swallowed up in the wind that shrieked in the rigging and none of the other members of the duty watch were aware of what had happened.

The saloon door had blown open, and Captain Sheppard, in his fall, struck its sharp edge before landing on a hatch. The force of the fall knocked the wind out of him and for a few moments he was lying, unconscious, on the deck rolling about.

The captain lay there for quite a while, unable to move. Finally with a great effort, he dragged himself inside the saloon and again collapsed on the floor. He was there some time before he was found by Able Seaman John Murrin, a member of the duty watch who was making his rounds, checking the stoves in the galley and the saloon. He helped Captain Sheppard to a chair and then raised the alarm. It wasn't too long before Captain Sheppard was being gently carried to his own cabin.

The first thing the chief steward did, after getting Captain Sheppard as comfortable as he could, was send for Commander Marr. He came, examined the captain, and gave as his opinion that Captain Sheppard had broken several ribs in the fall and perhaps received internal injuries. He got bandages and strapped the injured area. Captain Sheppard was still unable to get comfortable in his bunk, and the rolling and plunging of the ship caused him a great deal of pain. However, he made very little fuss and said he was sure he would be up and around in a few days.

During the night, I went to see him. He was having difficulty breathing, especially during spasms of pain. The next morning however, he was breathing much easier, as Commander Marr had loosened the bandages around his ribs. Later in the morning the weather cleared, the sun came out, the sea became calm and tranquil and we caught our first sight of land with King George Island's north foreland on our starboard bow, and Bridgeman Island's brown volcanic cone to port. The distant islands soon became clear and now we could navigate by sight.

When the seas abated Captain Sheppard was able to rest more easily, and directed the navigation of the *Eagle* from his sick bed. On Monday, January 29, we saw Deception Island, clearly visible ahead of us, our first port of call in Antarctica.

Deception Island, a volcano that is still slightly active is a very remarkable place. Circular in shape, the island is some nine miles in diameter and towers some 2,000 feet over the surrounding ocean. Its one eruption carved out part of its crater. When it had cooled it gave a natural entrance, called Neptune's Bellows, into the crater which forms the harbour known as the Bay of Whales.

At the turn of the century, Deception Island became a large whaling station, but during the war the whaling had been discontinued, and the extensive workshops, living quarters, kitchens and mess rooms had an air of desolation. In its heyday eight large whaling factory ships had often lain at anchor in the natural crater.

We steamed through Neptune's Bellows, and once inside the harbour were delighted to find the S.S. *Fitzroy* and H.M.S. *William Scoresby* lying at anchor. We noticed that

Entrance to the volcanic harbour at Deception Island.

they had already beached the oil barge that was to supply the *Scoresby* for her two year tour-of-duty in the Antarctic waters. The base established the year previously was in good shape and we had a lot of cargo to land there. As well, we were to load cargo from the *Fitzroy* and the *Scoresby* for the new base to be established at Hope Bay.

After we had anchored and got settled away, we went on board the other ships for a reunion. As soon as they learned of Captain Sheppard's accident, H.M.S. *Scoresby* was immediately dispatched to the base at Lockroy on Wiercke Island to bring back Dr. Black who was stationed there. He arrived a day later and confirmed Commander Marr's first diagnosis of broken ribs and possible internal injuries. Dr. Black strapped Captain Sheppard, but fearing complications from internal

"Skipper" Tom Carroll standing on an oil tank inside the volcano at Deception Island.

injuries, he advised the removal of Captain Sheppard to the hospital at Port Stanley in the Falkland Islands.

When Captain Sheppard was told of this plan, he pointed out that his removal from command of the S.S. *Eagle* would mean that she would have to return to Newfoundland and would not be able to take part in the Hope Bay expedition. He suggested that he stay with the *Eagle* until the Hope Bay base was established. It was a serious decision, but Captain Sheppard had his way and remained in charge of the ship. On the long voyage south, Captain Sheppard had won the respect and confidence of all the ship's company, and as we prepared for the last and most likely the most dangerous part of our mission, we would all rest easier knowing he was still in command.

Dr. Black also told Captain Sheppard he would rest much more comfortably in a softer bed. So, several eiderdown sleeping bags were sewn together to serve as a soft mattress and Captain Sheppard was soon resting much more comfortably.

We were all fascinated by Deception Island and could hardly believe that we were actually lying at anchor in the crater of a still-active volcano. There were no beaches as we knew them, nothing, only the smooth molten lava running down into the water. This lava was still warm, and after every snowstorm, the snow would melt away from it after a couple of hours.

All around the Bay of Whales there were signs of the former whaling activity. The tattered old shacks and the whale bones lying along the lava beaches bore mute witness to the great hunts of yesteryear. This had been the most southern whale oil factory in the world and the huge oil tanks were still in place. They were however, rendered useless by a British warship, which had been sent to blow up the tanks in 1941. At that time German ships were using Deception Island to refuel and take on fresh water. On one of the old tanks someone had painted an Argentinian flag, and a member of the *Eagle's* crew was sent to paint over it with a large square of red paint. Deception Island was to be under British jurisdiction and this was part of our mission, to re-establish British claims in Antarctica.

One of the most fascinating places on the island was the most southern cemetery in the world. Here were a number of monuments, mostly to the memory of Norwegian whalers who had lost their lives while hunting the whales in these waters.

Our stay at Deception Island was a busy one for our crew, for we had to sort out the cargo that had to be landed there

The most southern cemetry in the world is on Deception Island.

and take on cargo from the S.S. *Fitzroy* and H.M.S. *William Scoresby*. This took a couple of days to accomplish. The Huskies had been taken ashore and were waiting to be loaded onto the *Eagle* for their long voyage to Hope Bay.

It was at Deception Island that I made my first contact with the seal leopard, a vicious sea marauder that feeds on seals and penguins. They had no fear and would attack a man as quickly as a bird and had even been known to attack small boats. Needless to say, we tried to avoid contact with them, but the crew had to kill a few for food for the dogs. The seal leopard when hunted put up a vicious fight. Luckily we suffered no injuries from them.

At long last everything was sorted out, the dogs taken on board and we were ready to depart for our first task, that of supplying the existing bases before starting our main objective to enter Hope Bay, and land our scientist and their supplies. The outfitting of the two existing bases went smoothly, and on February we set sail for Hope Bay.

Chapter 12

Before we left Deception Island, the British scientific expedition suffered a great loss. Commander Marr, who had become ill, asked to be relieved of his duties so as not to ruin the mission's chances of success. He requested that Captain Andrew Taylor be appointed in his place. The Governor of the Falklands agreed, and Captain Taylor took command. We took a sad leave from Commander Marr who remained at the Deception Island base until his return to Port Stanley.

On February 11 we were given the order to proceed to Hope Bay. The weather was good as we hauled our anchor on board after a bit of a struggle, for it had fouled, and, we then prepared to leave Deception Island. Captain Sheppard now felt well enough to come to the bridge, and as we sailed down the inside harbour of Deception Island towards Neptune's Bellows, he took a last look at the old whaling station. Then he turned to me and said, "Well Sparks, looks like we're on the last leg of our journey, with everything shipshape. The oil barge is moored okay," and he pointed to it, "and the *William Scoresby* has a good two-year fuel supply." He stopped talking to watch the S.S. *Fitzroy* steam down the harbour on her way to Port Lockroy.

We looked more like a replica of Noah's Ark than a ship on a secret admiralty mission, especially with the twenty-five

View from bridge of S.S. Eagle *laden with cargo and dogs.*

dogs barking and howling. The dogs were tied up all over the ship's deck, wherever we could find a place to put them. Some were even put on board the scow lashed on the stern. Between the dogs and our strange and varied cargo, there wasn't room to put your feet down properly, but somehow we made do and carried on.

As we passed through Neptune's Bellows and out into the open ocean we found some signs of light ice, but nothing to give us any worry. With luck on our side Captain Sheppard thought we would make Hope Bay in about twenty hours and he was dead on.

We made it safely to Hope Bay and luck was with us. An offshore wind was blowing the ice offshore, so we had no

Glacier at Hope Bay

trouble getting near the shore where the expedition hoped to set up its base camp.

As we steamed into Hope Bay with its mile-wide entrance, I was standing on the bridge with Captains Sheppard and Taylor. It was a majestic sight that met our eyes. Two miles away at the head of Hope Bay stood a great valley glacier flanked by lateral moraines. On the north side was a very high mountain mass that ran down some three thousand feet to a flat area covered by a thick sheet of ice, and below at sea level were ice cliffs, eighty to one hundred feet in height. The southeastern side of the bay was quite different and was backed by a snow-free peak. Between it and the shore there were acres of pleasant hilly ground entirely devoid of ice and snow. It was obvious that the base huts should be erected somewhere on this ice-free site.

We had entered Hope Bay around 6.00 a.m. and cruised about the area until noon waiting for the southwest breeze that was blowing offshore to moderate before dropping anchor. After breakfast Captain Taylor called a conference with the members of the British expedition. He suggested they take a day or two to examine the snow-free area before choosing a campsite. They agreed.

The site had to be on level ground, near the sea, and close to a stream that could provide a good summer water supply. It was also very important for sanitary reasons that the base camp not be too near the large penguin rookery which was in the area. It didn't take them long to choose a site and it was just around the corner from where we had moored the S.S. *Eagle*.

Our anchorage was a small cove which we later renamed "Eagle Cove". It was on a lee shore but had very deep water and seemed like a safer berth for the old ship. We let out ninety fathoms of chain on what seemed to be a steep bottom, and secured the ship as best we could.

The prevailing winds at this time of the year seemed to be westerlies. Some small icebergs that had broken off from the main glacier occupied the cove close to where we had anchored. These bergs were a good source of water. Once the scow was launched, before landing any cargo, most of the crew were sent to collect ice from a small flat berg. Several scow loads were collected. This took the better part of a day, but Captain Sheppard felt it was important to replenish both our domestic tanks and the ship's boiler tanks. Vic Rumsey, Billy Bishop and Earle Hayes were part of the crew who were sent on this mission. They made light of their task and had a good many laughs about this strange way of replenishing our water supply.

Collecting ice in Hope Bay

That evening we had fresh seal for supper. One of the crew had shot it and brought it back to the ship. Then Skipper Tom Carroll, the veteran of sixty years at the ice, took over. The members of the expedition stood around watching in amazement as old Skipper Tom flensed the carcass. In ten minutes he had removed the heavy skin and layer of blubber, and the carcass was dressed and ready for the oven. Later, we found it took even the experienced seal skinners on board a good hour to do the same work. We all enjoyed the change from our usual diet of pork or mutton.

Later that night we had our first close call with the dangers of Antarctica. As we lay peacefully at anchor in Eagle Cove, all tuckered out after a busy day, a gale force wind sprang up and we were forced to use our engine to ease the strain on the *Eagle's* anchor chains for fear they would break. We were doing okay until later in the evening an iceberg bore down on us with considerable speed. We had no time to hoist the anchor, and there was absolutely nothing we could do, but watch with anxiety as the great mass of ice driven by the stiff offshore wind made its way towards us.

All hands were on the bridge, of course, and I heard Skipper Tom Carroll turn to Captain Sheppard and say in a quiet, unemotional voice, "Well Captain, I guess this is the end." But once again the luck of the old *Eagle* held, and just as it seemed we were doomed, the berg must have grounded for it stopped and turned to one side, and then moved to starboard.

Captain Sheppard, with the ship's engine going full out, saw his chance. He spun the wheel of the *Eagle*, and the old ship sheered away, letting the giant iceberg slide harmlessly past. Later, we thought how strange it was that the same source that provided our water supply could become so dangerous. This incident alerted Captain Sheppard and from that time on, there was always a man on watch to give warning of any approaching bergs.

The next day the wind died and we started unloading our cargo. The first to go ashore were the dogs. We put the twenty-five excited animals in the scow and carried them very close to the nearest point of land, then threw them overboard. They were excellent swimmers, and had no trouble making it ashore. Once ashore they headed for the large penguin rookery. To stop them plenty of seal meat had been placed near where they'd landed. By the time they had finished with the seal meat, they had been all rounded up and tied to a long rope, about ten feet apart. This kept them from attacking the penguins. The dogs were well fed and ate about four pounds of seal meat every other day.

Construction of base camp at Hope Bay.

Now that the dogs were safely landed, the scow was used to unload the rest of the *Eagle's* cargo and construction of the base camp at Hope Bay began.

CHAPTER 13

After we had secured ship in Eagle Cove, I decided it would be a good time to go ashore and have a closer look at the penguin rookery. I borrowed the ship's dory after old Skipper Tom Carroll and with the help of Robert Pittman and John Hayward, had checked our anchorage by means of the sounding line and rowed ashore.

It was very quiet this Antarctic evening, the only noise being the sound of the penguins returning home after a day's fishing. You could trace their arrival by the sound they made on landing. They would swim towards the shore with their heads underwater, occasionally coming up for air. They reminded me of dolphins as they came out of the water, jumping from the water to the edge of the shore ice, eager to clean their feathers before going on to feed their young in the rookery.

This particular rookery had about 50,000 Adélie penguins, as well as a small colony of Jentou penguins, about 500 in number. There were also a number of gulls, Antarctic terns, skuas and some large petrels.

As soon as they had dried their feathers the penguins would form a line and waddle up the steep path to the rookery, about seven hundred yards from the sea.

The author with penguins.

On arriving at the rookery the mother penguins would choose their own chicks without any difficulty and regurgitate the fish they had caught until it seemed the young ones had enough. Then the mothers would slide down the slope to the sea, and the young ones would give chase until they caught up with the mother who would then regurgitate more fish, and then keep going until the chicks caught up again, and the same thing would happen. This was the mother's way of helping the chicks digest the food they had taken.

I spent a pleasant time observing the ways of the penguins, and other Antarctic birds. In fact, in my spare time I often came back to the same spot, and never tired of watching the way of life in the rookery.

Of course, I didn't get to spend a lot of time ashore, for

until the expedition party had set up a radio system I was busy, as the S.S. *Eagle* was the main communication centre. I had to keep in contact with Port Lockroy and Deception Island, and relay all messages to Port Stanley in the Falkland Islands.

For the next two weeks all hands were busy unloading the supplies for the expedition. However, after our brush with the iceberg, we kept a constant lookout for danger and a duty watch was maintained twenty-four hours a day on the *Eagle*. In the meantime, the crew unloaded our cargo as quickly as they could, for we were aware that a change in weather could mean that we might have to cut and run without warning to the people ashore.

The first thing we did preparatory to unloading our cargo was to launch the huge old scow from our stern. It proved to be no easy matter with the *Eagle's* rusty old davits creeking and wrenching under the strain, but at last it was accomplished, and the work of unloading began.

The scow's first cargo was the temporary base hut so that the expedition could start to get set up onshore. Then for eighteen days, working long hours and dragging everything over treacherous terrain, the crew of the *Eagle* unloaded 400 tons of cargo.

Once the cargo was landed, we immediately got underway for the return voyage to Deception Island. Here we would take on a second load of cargo that had been stored there by the S.S. *Fitzroy*, and H.M.S. *William Scoresby*, for the return trip to Hope Bay.

We made good time on the 120-mile journey to Deception Island, and on March 2 once again passed through Neptune's Bellows and anchored in the calm waters of the volcano crater.

I had made radio contact with the people at the Deception Island base before our arrival, and they all came to greet us when we came to anchor. Their main generator had caught fire shortly after we had left on our first trip and they had had no radio contact with the expedition. So, they were anxious for news of how things were going back at Hope Bay, and more than glad to learn that the first part of our mission had been very successful, and the expedition now in place. We had brought a new generator and this restored their radio contact.

We really enjoyed a couple of days' rest, in fact it was only in this peaceful setting that we fully realized the strain that our stay in Hope Bay had put on us. It was not only the physical strain of landing cargo and pulling it over rough terrain but the mental strain of not knowing at what moment the icebergs might crush the old ship without any warning. It was a very stressful situation and every man was showing the effects of it.

The rest and relaxation at Deception Island did us good, and we enjoyed the well-cooked meals and the extra tot of rum that was served by Captain Sheppard for a job well done.

On March 3 we began the task of taking on the remaining cargo for our last trip to Hope Bay. Part of our cargo was 30 tons of coal. The coal had been put in bags, and these were brought out from shore in small dories, and then stowed below. We also had about 20 tons of lumber, which again had to be brought out, hoisted aboard, and carefully stored for the voyage back to Hope Bay. This lumber was to be used to replace the temporary hut erected for the expedition at Hope Bay. It was tedious, back-breaking work, but at last everything was stowed away and we were ready to sail.

As it was March month, the old-timers like Tom Carroll and other crewmembers, who had gone to the ice in the *Eagle*, remembered the sealing voyages of past years. When the day's work was finished there would be stories of bumper voyages, and the many narrow escapes from death that were part and parcel of the seal hunt. Little did any of us think, as we listened to these stories, that the greatest danger ever faced by the old *Eagle* lay ahead of us.

The weather was now starting to get stormy. The thermometer fell, and we had several blizzards that drove a fine powdery snow all over the ship and the island. The snow soon melted on the warm volcanic rock around the crater of Deception Island. However, it was clear that the winter season was coming to Antarctica, and we would be wise to complete our work if we wanted to get back to Port Stanley before the ice trapped us at Hope Bay.

Chapter 14

March 11, 1945 dawned clear and bright. We had finished loading cargo the day before, and were now ready to make our last run to Hope Bay. Once again we sailed out from Neptune's Bellows and Captain Sheppard set our course.

It was remarkable how fast the weather had changed in just a couple of weeks. Our return voyage to Hope Bay was much more difficult for drift ice was quickly filling Drake Passage and we had to proceed with due care and caution.

Captain Sheppard had anticipated some difficulty and had taken the precaution of taking on board a quantity of gun powder that had been left at Deception Island by the whalers some years previously. The gun powder would be used to loosen the ice around the *Eagle* if we should become stuck in the drift ice.

However, we didn't have to use the gun powder as the drift ice was loose enough and the stout old *Eagle* was able to force a passage through it, though, on a few occasions it was touch and go. We made it back safely and crept up to our old anchorage in Eagle Cove.

Captain Sheppard had calculated that as our fuel supply for the *Eagle* was getting low, we would have to be in Port Stanley by April 3. The fact that the quicker we could unload the cargo, the quicker we would be on our way to the

Antarctic icebergs

Falklands, gave the crew new energy and they set about unloading the second cargo with a will.

The weather remained fairly good until March 14, and we were able to land most of the cargo. However, a new danger now threatened for large icebergs began to break away from the main glacier, and we had to move the *Eagle* several times to escape being crushed. As a result, a crewmember had to be stationed in the bow to give warning of the breaking bergs.

It was a busy time for me as there were many radio messages to be relayed to Port Stanley and back to the other Antarctic outposts. As a result I had little time to think of the dangers that threatened us daily, and the days seemed to blend one into the other as the process of unloading cargo went on.

On shore, everything was going well and the new buildings to house the British expedition were under construction.

Chippie, our ship's carpenter, was directing operations and by March 14 the foundations for the new buildings were completed. However, the wind seemed to be constantly increasing and this made landing cargo difficult.

Friday, March 16, dawned fair with little wind and no snow. It was cold however, but good for landing cargo and getting on with the construction of the new huts. Three loads of cargo were landed, but then the glass began to fall, and there was snow. It was clear that a storm was on its way.

St. Patrick's Day, March 17, came unnoticed. Back home in Newfoundland there would be great celebrations but here it was just another work day. At daylight, even in the shelter of Hope Bay, the effects of an impending storm were soon evident.

My first warning that there was a problem came early in the morning. The bridge telegraphed the engine room demanding full speed ahead. Then, the steering chains that ran under my cabin floor began to race through their pulleys. The engine was still going full speed when a knock came on my door, and it opened to show Skipper Tom Carroll. "We've parted our anchors, Markie," he said with just a trace of concern in his voice, "and now we're trying to put to sea to ride out the storm. Captain Sheppard needs you on the bridge right away."

I immediately ran to the bridge. Captain Sheppard was a worried man. He told me that even with the *Eagle's* engine at full speed, the wind had forced her to drag her anchors and they had snapped under the strain, so that we were now drifting at the mercy of the elements. He told me to try and contact the shore base to let them know what was happening.

In the meantime, Captain Sheppard ordered the crew to cut loose the scow that was fastened to our stern for fear it would tangle with our rudder. Even with the *Eagle's* engine straining at full speed we had little or no way to manoeuvre and drifted along helplessly.

The storm was growing stronger by the moment and visibility in the driving snow was nil. I quickly made my way back to my cabin and set about contacting the shore base. (At first, I had no luck, for the "Walkie-Talkie" radio was off at the shore base.) As I was trying to contact the shore, without warning, all hell broke loose. The old ship lurched so violently that I was thrown against the cabin door and came face to face with old Skipper Tom Carroll who was just about to enter my cabin.

Skipper Tom was as near to tears as I had ever seen him come. He clutched my arm and roared over the howl of the wind, "We're going to lose her, Markie, we're going to lose her." The tears in Skipper Tom's eyes were not for himself—he had no fear of death—but for his beloved old ship, the *Eagle*.

I lifted my eyes at that moment and through a slight ease in the snow squalls saw a huge iceberg gliding past the *Eagle*. The iceberg had our bowsprit and part of our bow sticking out of it. Some of the rigging and a portion of the rail from the forecastle deck were also embedded in the ice. It was obvious we had collided with the berg and suffered serious structural damage.

At the sight of the iceberg Skipper Tom grabbed my arm and it was only by a stroke of luck I kept him from falling to the deck below. I was not so lucky, for in holding Skipper Tom back, I missed my own footing and fell to the deck below, landing with a great thump that shook every bone in my body.

To make matters worse, just as I landed, the *Eagle* rolled violently and I was in danger of being swept overboard. It was only by jamming my legs against the railing and holding on for dear life that I managed to keep my position.

Although badly shaken, I wasn't seriously hurt and with a bit of effort made it back to the wireless room. I was just inside the room when the *Eagle* scraped along the side of another iceberg. At this point, the shore base switched on their radio, and I made contact, telling them we had parted our anchors, and had to put to sea, and had suffered structural damage from the ice. I asked them to keep the radio on in case of other messages. Then I left the wireless room and went back to the bridge to report to Captain Sheppard. He told me we had collided with two icebergs. The first one tore away our bow, the second had scraped our side. With the prevailing weather conditions it was impossible to assess the total damage to the ship. In such a blizzard no one could venture on the foreward head to see what had happened. He asked me to go back to the wireless room and contact the shore base.

"Tell them," he said, "we've lost both our anchors and eighty fathoms of chain. We've hit two icebergs but can't assess the full extent of the damage we have suffered. We think we are somewhere south of the base. Ask them to stand by until we contact them again."

We knew our damages were serious for each time the *Eagle* dipped the ocean flooded into the forecastle, forcing the crew to seek shelter in the stern of the ship. Then, there was more bad news when the engine room reported flooding, and the pumps were unable to keep ahead of the water which was steadily rising.

This news came as I was leaving the bridge to try and contact the shore base again. When Captain Sheppard heard that the water was rising in the engine room, he made an instant decision.

"Cancel that first message to shore, Sparks," he said, "the situation has changed. Tell them we have no hope of weathering the storm, and I'm going to try and get her into Eagle Cove. Ask them to go there as quickly as they can, and bring ropes, and anything else that may help the crew get safely ashore."

My hopes for survival fell. Eagle Cove was a rocky beach strewn with boulders and the huge seas sweeping over our ship would tear her bottom out long before she was beached. I knew it was a hard decision to make, and either way death stared us in the face.

I went back to the wireless room, and although the storm made reception difficult, I managed to relay the Captain's message. They received it on shore, and answered that they were on their way to the Cove. A few minutes later Captain Sheppard sent for me to come back to the bridge. He had just gotten a bit of good news. The pumps in the engine room now seemed to be dealing with the water which had just started to recede.

At this point Captain Sheppard called all hands to the bridge and explained our situation. There were only two alternatives, stay with the *Eagle*, and hope the pumps would continue to handle the leaks until we made it back to Port Stanley in the Falkland Islands or attempt to beach her in Eagle Cove. He was of the opinion we should try and make it back to Port Stanley, and asked the officers and crew if they would trust to his judgement.

There was total agreement to try and make it back to Port Stanley for we all knew the dangers of trying to land at Eagle Cove. When the crew had spoken, Captain Sheppard turned to me and said, "Contact the shore Sparks, and tell them we're going to try and make it to Port Stanley."

Just as I made contact with the shore base, there came a change in the weather, the wind eased a bit and the snow stopped. Even as I gave the operator on shore our decision, he told me they could now see us turning our battered bow seaward and wished us Godspeed.

So, with Captain Sheppard on the bridge, and Skipper Tom Carroll standing beside him, short of fresh water, and with bunker running low, we began the long, slow trek to Port Stanley. But, there was hope, for we trusted Captain

Sheppard's judgement. As old Skipper Tom Carroll said, the *Eagle* had weathered many an Arctic gale in her forty years at the northern ice fields, and he was sure she'd do as she always had done, and bring her crew safely home.

As far as I was concerned we now had a chance of survival, while if we had had to beach her, few of us would have survived. It was still however, touch and go, for with the winds still at gale force we could do little to repair the damages we had suffered. All we could do was limp along and wait for the weather to settle.

Temporary repairs to the bow of the S.S. Eagle *made at sea after collision with iceberg.*

The next day the storm abated, the sun came out, and we got the chance we had been waiting for, to try and make some temporary repairs. Under the leadership of Skipper Tom Carroll, we collected every spare blanket and sleeping bag and stuffed them into the gaping hole the iceberg had punched in our bow. Chippie the carpenter, was lowered over the bow in a bo'sun's chair to try and stretch a canvas shield over the damaged area. Twice, as the *Eagle* dipped into the waves, Chippie was thrown back onto the deck, but undaunted by the waves, went over the bow again to continue his work. Before the day was over, the canvas shield was in place and our chances of survival greatly increased.

Normally it would have been a three-day voyage to Port Stanley. In our crippled condition, Captain Sheppard took no chances, and when a storm blew up, he swung the *Eagle* stern into the wind to lessen the chances of further damage to the bow. It took us seven days to make Port Stanley, and with every mile closer to our destination, our spirits rose, and our hope of making it to Port Stanley slowly increased.

H.M.S. William Scoresby

Finally on Victoria Day, May 24, 1945, under the escort of H.M.S. *William Scoresby* which came to our assistance, we entered Port Stanley. A large crowd hearing of our heroic fight for survival came down to the dock to welcome us. We were all happy now for as old Skipper Tom had said, the luck of the *Eagle* had held, and the 6,000-mile homeward voyage had really begun.

CHAPTER 15

While waiting for temporary repairs at Port Stanley, we had plenty of time to think about the series of adventures and misadventures that had been our lot since leaving Newfoundland nearly seven months earlier. Our most terrifying experience had been the near loss of the *Eagle* in Hope Bay. It was only the excellent seamanship of the captain and crew that had brought us back safely to the haven of Port Stanley. Yet, despite the dangers and hardships we had endured, we could take pride in the fact that Operation "Tabarin" had been successfully concluded with the British scientific expedition being established in Hope Bay. This had not been done without a price, and the captain and some of our crew bore the marks of the dangers encountered on our voyage.

Mr. Butler, our First Officer, had been the first victim and we had to leave him in hospital in a South American town on our inward voyage. This had been followed by John Power, one of our firemen, having to be hospitalized and left behind in Recife following a ship-board accident. Then, Victor Rumsey, Maxwell Rowe, John Heywood, Chief Engineer Lewis, Mr. Whitten and John Morris all had short stays in hospitals in various seaports, but luckily were able to rejoin the *Eagle* and continue on the voyage south-north.

Captain Sheppard had not been hospitalized, but his ship-board accident took its toll and it was a measure of the man's determination that he was able to finish that difficult and dangerous voyage.

We remembered, too, how Commander Marr had had to give up his dream of Antarctic exploration because of his illness and the terrible disappointment this must have been to him. When we thought of all these things we wondered what might lie ahead of us on the voyage home.

Temporary repairs to S.S. Eagle *at Port Stanley*

Our stay at Port Stanley was uneventful except that the whole crew of the *Eagle* were laid low by a bout of influenza, and had to keep to their beds for a week. In the meantime, temporary repairs were made to the *Eagle's* bow by filling it with concrete. This would make her more seaworthy for the voyage to Montevideo where she was to undergo a complete refit before attempting the voyage back to St. John's. Then, on March 31, on the eve of our departure for Montevideo we found out that dangers still lurked in these southern waters.

It was a fine evening and I went out on the deck to get a breath of fresh air. The harbour of Port Stanley was a peaceful scene. The S.S. *Fitzroy* was taking on cargo for her normal run to the outlying islands. Nearby was H.M.S. *Scoresby* getting a clean-up from her Antarctic voyage. I looked towards the *Eagle's* bow, now blocked with a glob of cement and thought about that awful morning in Hope Bay when old Skipper Tom Carroll and I watched in horror as the clipper bow of our ship drifted by, lodged in an iceberg. Then I went back to my cabin, grateful that we had survived and totally unaware that the elements were preparing to make one last attempt to claim the gallant *Eagle*.

Unknown to us, a tight and very deep depression was forming just west of the Andes Mountains, and on the first of April, without warning, it came down full force on Port Stanley Harbour.

We were supposed to sail at dawn, but a gale force wind kept us at our anchorage. By noon it was gusting to well over one hundred miles an hour. Shortly thereafter, we were in trouble again as the *Eagle* began snapping lines under the pressure of the wind and waves. In fact, all the lines parted except one, and we expected it to go any minute, as the old ship reared and plunged in the trough of the waves.

Then, at the height of the storm, Captain Sheppard had another narrow escape from death. He went to the bow to assess the situation, and a gust of wind took him and he was blown off the forecastle deck into the forward hold. He was badly shaken up, but suffered no serious injuries.

Luckily for us the single cable held and by late afternoon the winds subsided. Once again the *Eagle* had held her own against the cruel sea. However, it was a sharp reminder to us that even though Antarctica was behind us, we were still vulnerable to the fury of the elements.

The storm delayed our departure from Port Stanley, and it was not until April 11 that we said good-bye to the large crowd that came down to wish us Godspeed on our journey home. "Homeward goes the sailor" is an old proverb, and although we were sad to leave the many friends we had made at Port Stanley, deep down we were happy to continue on our way. On April 17, exactly one month after the near disaster at Hope Bay we again steamed past the wreck of *Graf Spee* on our way to Montevideo. Six days later we made port, and were welcomed at dockside by Mr. Butrell and Ted Allison of the firm of McClean and Stapleton, our ship's agents in Montevideo. Big Al, the manager of the Liberty Inn was there too, with Charlie, whom we had come to call our guardian angel, for he kept us out of trouble and made sure we had a memorable stay during our January sojourn in that fair city. They had all heard about our ordeal in Hope Bay, and the near disaster that had befallen us, and came to see our cement bow and hear the details of our brush with death.

We were to be at Montevideo for approximately the next three months. The *Eagle* was to go on drydock and have major repairs to restore her to her original condition—including her clipper bow. The *Eagle's* clipper bow was important to me, for it was the one feature of the old ship I had admired the first time I had seen her tied up at Mudges, when I went for my interview with Captain Sheppard. "A dirty, black, old worn-out wooden steamer with a clipper bow," had been my first impression, but I had long since come to feel that the old S.S. *Eagle* was something more than just a ship. Now she was my ship, and I wanted her to be whole again with her clipper bow restored. In fact, whenever I looked at the cement block where the bow had been, I remembered the *Eagle's* historic meeting with the last of the great old sailing barques, the *Lawhill*, and she too had a clipper bow. The one moment of that awful storm in Hope Bay that Skipper Tom Carroll and I would never forget, was seeing her clipper bow embedded in that iceberg. Like Skipper Tom, to whom the S.S. *Eagle* was home, I was happy she was about to be restored.

S.S. Eagle *on drydock at Montevideo*

When the *Eagle* went on drydock all the crew were sent ashore to a hotel. This was a nice break for all of us—a holiday of sorts. It was almost like a holiday, but each day we reported for work aboard the *Eagle*. Captain Sheppard used the occasion to try and get some rest. So, whenever his duties would allow, he stayed in bed as this was what the Spanish doctors of Montevideo had suggested. I visited him at his hotel almost daily and was of some help to him with the ship's clerical work. As well, I accompanied him to the *Eagle* whenever he had to make a survey of the work completed. After a week or so, the Captain began to feel better but he still found it difficult to get about without gasping for breath.

The Spanish doctors assured him that his breathing would improve as his general health improved. Captain Sheppard looked forward eagerly to the time when he would be well again and as the doctors had said, he slowly but surely improved as the days passed.

Chapter 16

We really enjoyed our stay in Montevideo, especially the weekends, for it meant more Saturday picnics and trips to the country from the Liberty Inn, with Charlie looking after us. These were feasts to be remembered, and what we all enjoyed most was when they sang "Roll Out The Barrel," and out she rolled, filled with the best of beer. We stood in line with our pint beer mugs, and drank to the honour and glory of all the Allied sailors, but especially for the Newfoundland sailors wherever they might be. Then there were the great singsongs on the way back to our hotel. All the old sea shanties, and some of the new, and the man of the hour was the one who could render the funniest ditty. The Sunday church parade came the following morning and all hands went to the service of their choice. Much to our surprise many of the different churches held their services in English.

On Monday it was back to the *Eagle*. However, there was a bit of a problem for there wasn't a lot to do while she was on drydock. Captain Sheppard solved this problem by having the men paint and do up the forecastle. "Do what you like," he said. "Paint, build new lockers, do whatever you think will spruce the old girl up a bit."

The crewmembers and firemen, to whom the forecastle was home, entered into the spirit of the work with a will.

They scrubbed, painted, built new lockers and when they were finished the forecastle was certainly a far cry from the dingy old place it had been.

When we were just about ready to sail for home, Captain Sheppard gave the crew an opportunity to get new fitouts of clothing and had the cost deducted from their wages. The crew were delighted for now they would arrive home to their wives and sweethearts in fine style.

While the *Eagle* was on drydock, Captain Sheppard arranged to have the deck scraped, and the forty-odd years' accumulation of pitch and blubber was at last removed. This made the return voyage through the tropics much more bearable. Still, when I looked at the *Eagle*, resplendent in her new state, I thought what a shame it was that next spring she would again be heading for the Arctic seal hunt, to once again be covered in seal skins and blubber.

While she was on drydock Chief Engineer Lewis suggested to the captain that now would be a good time to put a new bed under the main engine. It appeared that the flooding in Hope Bay had softened the wooden bed under the engine so much so that eventually the engine would sink into the wood and cause problems with the main propeller shaft alignment.

Now for the first time the cause of the friction between Captain Sheppard and Chief Lewis over the matter of engine speed was explained. It appeared that over the years the engine had been sinking slowly into the bed and Chief Lewis had been forced to keep putting wedges under the engine to keep it even. However, even with the wedges, the old bed could only hold the engine steady up to a certain speed. When this speed was exceeded the engine vibrated so badly that there was a real danger the main propeller shaft would crack. As a safety precaution a governor had been fixed to keep the engine below the speed that caused vibration and the governor could not be adjusted. This was why, Chief

Lewis explained to Captain Sheppard, he had not been able to increase speed during the time of danger in Hope Bay. This explanation gave Captain Sheppard a new respect for his chief engineer who had accomplished so much under this restriction.

The repairs on the *Eagle* went well, and it was a joy to all of us who had shared the dangers of Hope Bay, to see her back to the original design with the clipper bow fully restored. It meant, too, that soon we would be homeward bound.

A week before we were to embark for home, we decided to host a party for all our friends at the Liberty Inn. This would give us a chance to return the hospitality shown by our ship's agents and the personnel of the Liberty Inn. It would be a Newfoundland party paid for by the entire crew of the *Eagle*. We arranged for Al at the Liberty Inn to buy us a large pig which was then roasted on a spit. We also purchased a barrel of beer. The idea was that anyone who came to the Inn would be our guest. This was our way of saying thank you to the many people who had made our stay in Montevideo so pleasant.

When all was ready the party began. We rolled out the barrel, we served the roast pig, and we entertained. I think the most vivid memory I have of that "Newfoundland party" is Jimmy Hearn's beautiful rendition of "If You Ever Go Across the Sea to Ireland". He had a superb voice and all our guests were enthralled with his singing.

The party was a huge success, and on June 24, 1945—St. John's Day—we slipped our cables and began the long trek home. Rio was to be our next port of call where we would replenish our bunker coal. It was with mixed feelings that we saw Montevideo slip below the horizon—joy that we were at long last on our homeward voyage, and sadness at leaving behind the many friends we had made there.

We had an excellent passage to Rio de Janeiro but here tragedy struck again. One of our firemen, Nick Cullen, who was on shore leave was injured in a freak accident. As a result, he received a severe head injury. We were notified of the incident and Captain Sheppard took Nick to the port doctor for treatment. After examining the injury the doctor said that it wasn't too serious and he could continue the voyage. However, several days later while we were at sea, complications set in and he became critically ill.

Captain Sheppard took immediate action and gave me a message to send to the authorities at Bahia in Brazil, explaining why we had to enter that port. Then, we bore up for Bahia to get Nick into hospital as quickly as possible. He didn't make it. Just as we entered the harbour of Bahia, Nick died from the injuries he had received in the shore accident.

This tragedy was a terrible shock to all of us. After all we had been through, we had not lost a man. Now, death had claimed one of us. The death of a messmate at sea is a terrible thing. On a ship all hands must of necessity live in close contact, and a bond is forged so that death on a ship is everyone's personal tragedy. The empty seat in the galley, and the empty bunk in the forecastle were constant reminders of the loss.

It was impossible to bring Nick's body home for burial, so Captain Sheppard arranged for his burial in a cemetery in Bahia. We all went to his funeral and it was very memorable. We left our old messmate in a beautiful resting place high on a hillside overlooking the sea. We all agreed it was a fitting place for a sailor to sleep his last long sleep.

We left Bahia on August 5, and as we sailed out of the harbour, those of us who could lined the *Eagle's* rail for one last look at our comrade's resting place. It was a sad and sombre occasion, and I think it struck home to all of us when Dinny Hearn said in a loud voice to one of his shipmates, "Well mate, that's three down, wonder what's going to happen next?" Each of us looked, from one to another, and privately asked the same question. I think at that moment we realized we were still a long way from home with many miles to go.

Still, the sombre mood didn't last long. Sailors live in the present and we had work to do. It was a beautiful day, and we were now bound for our next port of call, the ancient Brazilian seaport of Pernambuco, now known as Recife. There we would refill our bunkers with coal for the return voyage up the South American coast.

CHAPTER 17

We had an uneventful voyage up the coast of South America; being a much more pleasant trip without the stench of blistering pitch and blubber. Our last port of call before leaving on the final leg of the journey home was the great city of New York. Here we tied up at the "Bowery" on the New York waterfront. We enjoyed our stay in New York but all hands were anxious for a sight of our island homeland. It was with great happiness we sailed from the Bowery, for Mudges the oldest dockside in St. John's. Mudges, by the way, got its name from an early English merchant who had a fishing and trading "room" there in the early eighteenth century. The premises were later bought by a St. John's firm, Bowring Brothers, the owners of the S.S. *Eagle*.

So we left the Bowery in high spirits and headed out Long Island Sound for home. It was a good voyage and with a ringing cheer from the crew, we entered the Narrows and docked at Mudges. The southern voyage of the S.S. *Eagle* had been successfully completed. However, for the *Eagle's* captain and crew there was to be a return trip to Antarctica to bring the British scientific expedition back from Hope Bay.

This time it was the turn of the M.V. *Trepassey*, one of the "Clarenville Fleet", so called because she had been locally built in the Clarenville shipyard. It would be the first time a Newfoundland-built ship, commanded by a Newfoundland captain and manned by a Newfoundland crew, would make a voyage to Antarctica.

The third week in November, 1945, the M.V. *Trepassey* sailed out the Narrows carrying us back to Antarctica. This time I had no worries about our radio capabilities as the *Trepassey* had been fitted with the very latest equipment. We also carried fifty-five Labrador Husky dogs in pens built on the deck of the ship, to be delivered to Hope Bay. As well, the *Trepassey* was laden with drums of kerosene oil for the Port Hope base and a large supply of dog food.

Once again ill luck dogged us on our voyage through the tropics. There was no bubbling blubber, but the dog food in the hold of the *Trepassey* went bad and the stench from the rotting dog food was just as terrible. The dogs kept escaping from their pens, making the lives of the crewmembers miserable. However, we cleaned the ship and at Pernambuco took on a new supply of dog food. In Montevideo we had the ship fumigated and cleaned before taking on supplies for the expedition at Hope Bay. Here we were also joined by seven persons, replacements for the expedition members who would be returning on the *Trepassey*.

We arrived at Port Stanley on New Year's Eve, 1945, and were welcomed by our old friends. They were especially glad to see us, as we were carrying their supply of Christmas turkeys, including one for the governor.

We left Port Stanley the first week in January and travelled to Deception Island where we began the task of delivering the supplies to the several Antarctic bases. The weather held, and with continuous daylight we made great progress and landed the supplies on schedule. Around the end of March, with a load of mail from the bases and the personnel who were being replaced, we set sail again for a return to civilization. But that is another story.

In 1949, I gave up going to sea and took a job on land. However, every time I looked across the harbour of St. John's and saw the old *Eagle* tied up at Mudges, I remembered the thrilling days when she carried us South on our great adventure.

Glenmount *(left)*; *S.S.* Eagle *(centre)*; Ice Hunter *(right)*

In the spring of 1950, Bowring Brothers decided the *Eagle* was no longer seaworthy and it was decided to scuttle her outside the Narrows. July 23, 1950 is a day many older Newfoundlanders will always remember, for it marked the last voyage of the S.S. *Eagle*, a short voyage to her final resting place off Sugar Loaf, just outside the Narrows of St. John's Harbour. I sat with my wife, Jean, and a host of other people on Signal Hill to see the gallant old ship go under.

Proudly, with all flags flying, she was towed from her berth at Mudges, travelling past Fort Amherst for the last time. She reached her last resting place and then we watched

S.S. Eagle

in silence as she began to slowly settle in the water. Suddenly she took a violent dip and her stern went under. As her stern slipped beneath the waves, her clipper bow that had braved many dangers stood upright. With her signal flags still fluttering in the breeze, it was the last we saw of the old, wooden-walled sealing steamer—a fitting end for such a gallant ship. Her memory will endure forever.

EPILOGUE

Antarctica is a continent of great size, equal almost to Europe and Australia put together, yet it has no permanent inhabitants. Only those who man weather and wireless or radio communication stations, and the bases from which parties of explorers set out, live there. Some go, only for one year, many for two, but never longer, unless the ship which is to take them out cannot reach their base. In that event, they must make the best of it and settle down to another year's work.

Of this vast continent, only about one percent is exposed rock; the remainder is covered with a mantle of snow and ice which varies from a few feet to as much as two miles in depth. In all, there are over 5,000,000 square miles covered in ice. This ice-covered area has a tremendous cooling effect on the air which moves over it. It is true to say that the Antarctic controls the weather of the Southern hemisphere.

The sea around the Antarctic freezes during the winter months from April to October, making it impossible for ships to reach the coast; but in the summer most of the ice breaks up forming fields of ice floes which move with the winds and currents.

This voyage to the bottom of the world required a lot of preparation and it was obvious that the crew were hand-picked by Captain Sheppard. They took delight in whatever they did; they never asked questions, but went on with their assignments, and were aware that this was not an ordinary trip to sea. The voyage was headed by the British Admiralty of London, England.

The S.S. *Eagle* was chosen as the expedition ship mainly because of her excellent ability to manoeuvre in ice. She had a well-constructed bow with steel plating. Her sides were completely sheathed with greenhart hardwood. With Captain Sheppard in command, we all felt that this was to be a voyage and experience that could not be missed for anything.

Crew Personnel

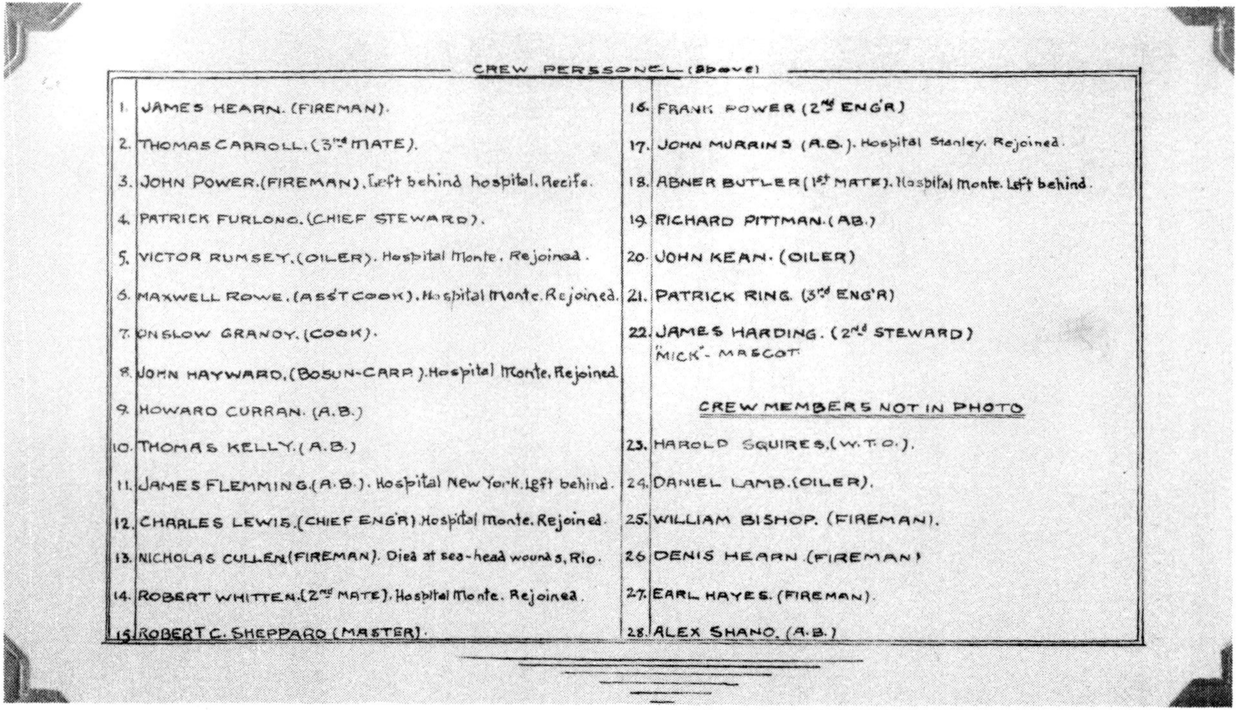

CREW PERSSONEL (above)

1. JAMES HEARN. (FIREMAN).
2. THOMAS CARROLL. (3rd MATE).
3. JOHN POWER. (FIREMAN). Left behind hospital. Recife.
4. PATRICK FURLONG. (CHIEF STEWARD).
5. VICTOR RUMSEY. (OILER). Hospital Monte. Rejoined.
6. MAXWELL ROWE. (ASS'T COOK). Hospital Monte. Rejoined.
7. ONSLOW GRANDY. (COOK).
8. JOHN HAYWARD. (BOSUN-CARP.). Hospital Monte. Rejoined.
9. HOWARD CURRAN. (A.B.)
10. THOMAS KELLY. (A.B.)
11. JAMES FLEMMING. (A.B.). Hospital New York. Left behind.
12. CHARLES LEWIS. (CHIEF ENG'R) Hospital Monte. Rejoined.
13. NICHOLAS CULLEN (FIREMAN). Died at sea-head wounds, Rio.
14. ROBERT WHITTEN. (2nd MATE). Hospital Monte. Rejoined.
15. ROBERT C. SHEPPARD (MASTER).
16. FRANK POWER (2nd ENG'R)
17. JOHN MURRINS (A.B.). Hospital Stanley. Rejoined.
18. ABNER BUTLER (1st MATE). Hospital Monte. Left behind.
19. RICHARD PITTMAN. (AB.)
20. JOHN KEAN. (OILER)
21. PATRICK RING. (3rd ENG'R)
22. JAMES HARDING. (2nd STEWARD)
"MICK" - MASCOT

CREW MEMBERS NOT IN PHOTO

23. HAROLD SQUIRES. (W.T.O.).
24. DANIEL LAMB. (OILER).
25. WILLIAM BISHOP. (FIREMAN).
26. DENIS HEARN. (FIREMAN)
27. EARL HAYES. (FIREMAN).
28. ALEX SHANO. (A.B.)

Captain Robert C. Sheppard, M.B.E.

A man of high calibre and experience. Prior to being Harbour Master of St. John's he was a square-rigger captain, having a Foreign-going Masters ticket which allowed him to sail on any class ship of his choice. He was favourably known in Britian for having convoyed confiscated Vichy-French ships across the Atlantic after the fall of France.

Captain Abe Butler

A foreign-going skipper, both in sail or steam, he was also a man of high qualities, in seamanship and navigation. Captain Abe was our Chief Officer.

Robert W. Whitten

A seaman with Arctic experience, he was a member of the famed Balbo-Labrador expedition. Mr. Whitten was to be our Second Officer.

Thomas Carroll

Normally the Eagle's full-time caretaker and bo'sun, he would become the Third Officer. He was a member of the Perry and Bartlett expedition to the North Pole in 1908-1909. At the time of our voyage to the Antarctic he was eighty-one years of age.

Charles Lewis

A long-time engineer with the firm of Bowring Brothers Ltd., and as far as I can determine, was one of the first recipients of a Chief Engineer's Marine Licence in Newfoundland.

Frank Power

A veteran of coal-fired steam engines, Frank left the comforts of a large marine repair shop to join the *Eagle* for the adventure to the bottom of the world as Second Engineer.

Patrick Ring

A long-time engine room companion of the chief's, Mr. Ring knew the *Eagle's* engine from the boilers to the smokestack. Mr. Ring was to be our Third Engineer.

John Hayward

Nicknamed "Chippie", John signed on as Ship's Carpenter and Bo'sun. The *Eagle*, being a wooden ship, required constant attention, and that was a full-time job.

Deckhands and Seamen

Howard Currin
Alex Shano
Richard Pittman
John Murrin
James Fleming
Thomas Kelly

Firemen and Oilers

Victor Rumsey
Danny Lamb
Jackey Kean
William Bishop
Earl Hayes
James Hearn
Nichlos Cullen
John Power
Dennis (Dinny) Hearn

Stewards and Cooks ———

Patrick (Nick) Furlong, Chief Steward
James Harding, Second Steward
Onslow Grandy, First Cook
Maxwell Rowe, Second Cook

Wireless Officer and Purser ———

Harold W. Squires (Author)

Harold Squires

Harold W. Squires was born on June 23, 1923 at St. John's, Newfoundland, into the family of Frederick and Maude Squires. He grew up and was educated in St. John's.

In 1940 he went to sea at the early age of 17, and served on several ships on the North Atlantic convoys during the Second World War.

Deciding to better his sea-going career, the following year he attended wireless training and became a certified Radio Officer, under the auspices of Canadian Marconi Co.

He was assigned his first ship in 1941, the S.S. *Moyra* which was later destroyed by fire. His next assignment was on a wooden sealing ship, the S.S. *Eagle*, which went on an exciting and dangerous secret mission for the British Admiralty to Antarctica—about which this book is written.

In 1949 he became a Federal civil servant as an employment officer with the National Employment Service, until his retirement in 1987.

At present he resides in St. John's and continues to operate his own amateur radio station as VOIDM.